INNOVATIVE
GRANDPARENTING

INNOVATIVE GRANDPARENTING

How Today's Grandparents Build Personal Relationships with Their Grandkids

Karen O'Connor

Copyright © 1995 Concordia Publishing House
3558 S. Jefferson Avenue, St. Louis, MO 63118-3968
Manufactured in the United States of America

Library of Congress Cataloging-in-Publication Data

O'Connor, Karen, 1938–

    Innovative Grandparenting / Karen O'Connor
       p.   cm.
    ISBN 0-570-04824-9
    1. Grandparenting.   I. Title.
HQ759.9.O26 1995
306.874'5—dc20   95–10024

1 2 3 4 5 6 7 8 9 10   04 03 02 01 00 99 98 97 96 95

Dedicated to my grandfather Gerald,
who taught me about being a
"great" grandparent long before I became one.

"Children's children are a crown
to the aged, and parents are the pride
of their children."
Proverbs 17:6

CONTENTS

Part 3
The Tough Issues: Living with Challenges

Part 4
Let Go and Let God

A NOTE FROM THE AUTHOR

Tucked away in the minds of many today is a loving memory (or fantasy) of a grandmother in a flower-print apron busily preparing a multi-course Thanksgiving dinner or whipping up a batch of chocolate chip cookies, eager to enfold her grandchildren in her full, soft arms at any time of the day or night.

Grandpa, on the other hand, is a friendly handyman who can fix a bike in a flash, tell a yarn a mile long about the old days, milk a cow, and bounce a crying baby on his knee.

Some grandparents today still fit that picture—and blessed are those grandchildren who have access to them. But what about grandmas who can't, don't want to, or no longer bake? Or who order out for Thanksgiving dinner? Or grandpas who can't pound a nail straight, have never seen a cow face to face, or who feel nervous or inadequate around babies under six months? Can they, too, be upstanding members of the Grandparents' Club?

I hope so because I'm a grandmother who rarely bakes and who no longer eats meat. In fact, I plan to order the Thanksgiving turkey (for the rest of the family) from a nearby restaurant. But my grandkids can count on me for a good game of Shadow Tag, Junior Monopoly, or Candyland. And I'm a great story-reader, skit producer, and all-around climber (hills, cliffs at the beach, or mountains)!

My husband, Grandpa Charles, on the other hand, is the handyman grandfather who can fix anything and is not a bit reserved around children of any age. In fact, most of the time, you'll find him crawling on the floor after the toddlers and rocking an infant to sleep in front of the television. He's also a great cook and does laundry and ironing to perfection.

Perhaps as you read this you're clicking off in your mind your preferences and strengths as a grandparent. If so, keep going. I think it's important for us to see ourselves as honestly as we can—and to count it all good. There is no one way to behave as a grandparent. We come in many different "packages." And each of us has something special to give our grandchildren, whether traditional or current in style and approach.

My hope is, that as you read this book, you will discover how best to

- express your full self as a grandparent—without guilt;

- experience the joy of being a grandparent—without restraint;

- explore new dimensions of grandparenting—without fear.

To help you accomplish this, I have divided the book into four parts. In Part 1, I focus on who we are, our differences and similarities, lifestyles and values. You will meet a number of grandparents—many I hope you can relate to, men and women who want to be an integral part of the lives of their grandchildren.

In Part 2, these grandparents talk about ways to make memories with grandchildren, build traditions, spend time together, handle long-distance relationships, and share spiritual values.

Part 3 deals with the tough issues: the challenges faced by grandparents who raise grandchildren, how divorce or death can change a relationship, and handling difficult communications with grandchildren and their parents.

Part 4 focuses on Spirit-filled grandparenting, as well as when and how to let go so God can do His perfect work in their lives and ours.

Finally, my wish for all of us is that we really know that God is with us as men and women, and as parents and grandparents. If so, who then can be against us?

Karen O'Connor

PART 1

GRANDPARENTS TODAY: WHO ARE WE?

1

OVER THE HIGHWAY AND THROUGH THE TRAFFIC ...

To grandmother's condo we go! A slight variation on the traditional song, but one that fits the status of many grandparents. For example, when my mother and father sold their home 14 years ago and moved to a high-rise apartment in a Chicago suburb, I remember my mother saying words to that effect. And I felt the shift in the status quo of our family.

Even though I was an adult with children of my own and living hundreds of miles away, I experienced a loss. I knew we would never again be together in that big house on Northwood Road that I had loved so much. Going to Grammy's and Bapa's wouldn't be the same. My children were sad as well.

It meant saying good-bye to traditions we had grown up with and brought into the next generation—picnics in the big backyard, snoozing on the swing in the screened-in porch, holiday parties in the cozy living room with a roaring fire, sleeping in the same room I had shared with my sister June.

It also meant saying good-bye to shoveling snow, mowing the lawn, repairing the roof, and painting the shutters. None of us missed that part!

Today, my children are grown with families of their own. Now I am a grandparent. And my life, like that of my parents before me, has taken its own twists and turns over the past decade. I no longer live in the house where I raised my children. I am no longer married to my children's father. I have a profession, and I work at it every day. I've also taken to the mountains in my free time. I love to hike and back-pack in the Sierra. And I am remarried and live in another city in a condominium.

My front "yard" is a bird and wildlife sanctuary on Mission Bay in San Diego, California. The play area for my grandchildren is a public park, and our "family room" is the multi-purpose recreation room on the first floor of our building. Life here is comfort-able and easy to maintain. But it's different—very dif-ferent from the lifestyle and expectations of grand-parents and grandchildren of a generation or two ago.

Grandparents' Club: Membership Open

Can those of us who don't fit the stereotype still be upstanding members of the Grandparents' Club with the same rights and privileges as those of previous generations? I say a resounding yes!

As I look at my friends who are grandparents, I see there is no one way to be or to behave. In fact, there seems to be a freedom available today that grandparents of yesterday might not have experienced or dared express. Lucky for us! We get to have a life, as the saying goes, and still be grandparents. One doesn't exclude the other.

My husband and I, as well as many of our friends, are discovering how to be great grandparents and step-grandparents—without guilt. We can be who we are right now. Stereotypes are out. Individuals are in. You can be who you are and still be a "great" grandmother or grandfather—whether you live in a trailer or a tent, in a condo or a cottage, in a hotel or a house.

The important things haven't changed, namely the presence of a grandparent in the life of a child, *your* presence in the life of *your* grandchildren.

Who We Are

With freedom, however, comes responsibility. Being a grandparent involves a lot more than where we live, what we do for a living, and how we express our individuality. Of primary importance to our children's children is who we are in our relationship with them. Our grandchildren are not impressed with our professional credentials, the state of our housing, or the fact that we have an enviable tomato garden. They are most interested in us as grandparents.

Following are some of the ways our children and grandchildren value us as grandmothers and grandfathers.

We depend on God's grace.

"Mom, I can't talk right now. I called to ask you to pray."

My friend Lee shared with me that, just as she had come in from work, her daughter Janet had phoned. Her voice shook as she relayed the news to Lee. Lee's eight-year-old granddaughter, Margie, flew off her bicycle while jumping a curb, and she had blacked out.

"We're at the hospital now," said Janet. "I'll call you as soon as I know something."

Lee immediately phoned me and other members of a prayer group to which we belonged. Janet later told her mother what comfort it gave her to know that Lee and others would begin praying right away.

"I can always count on you to keep the lines open between our family and God," she said gratefully.

Our children and our grandchildren often look to us when they need prayer. Even my son, who professes he isn't sure about the nature or presence of

God, was quick to phone me for prayer when a friend was in a life-threatening water-skiing accident.

And years ago, when my grandchildren and their parents lived abroad for a time, I realized that my greatest gift to them was daily prayer.

"My grace is sufficient for you, for my power is made perfect in weakness" (2 Cor. 12:9).

We express love.

"You ought to close the door on him. A kid on drugs is a disgrace to your family."

When Bob heard those words from a person he had thought was his friend, he cringed. How could he give up on 17-year-old Bobby—his one grandson, the boy who was named after him, the kid he had held, rocked, baby-sat for, camped with, and watched grow up?

Bob said he had suspected Bobby was into something—alcohol or drugs—but he resisted finding out the truth. "I noticed him withdrawing over the past year. He didn't come to family dinners as often, and when I invited him to a game or just to hang out together, he was always busy. And he seemed nervous and short-tempered when I did see him.

"Then his mother told me he was called in for drugs at school. It was one of the blackest days of my life. Not my Bobby. I couldn't let it in."

Bob recalled the day his grandson enrolled in a

treatment program. "It seemed like everyone in the family was in pieces that day—you know, an only child, only grandson. The spotlight had been on him from the time he was a baby. I wonder if that had something to do with why he went to drugs? Maybe he couldn't take the pressure. I don't know. But I love this boy. And I'm going to keep on showing him that I love him. And I'm gonna tell him too."

"*Love never fails*" (1 Cor. 13:8).

We value relationships.

One of the many things I love and respect about my mother and father as grandparents is the way they value each member of our family. Even now, with five great-grandchildren added to their quiver, they remain as interested and receptive as ever. In fact, just this week, I received a note from my mother thanking me for a letter I had sent updating her on my children and grandchildren. She shared a bit of news and then ended by telling me what a wonderful mother I am. What a lift that gave me.

And my children continue to keep in touch with her and my dad, even though they are many miles apart. They know that she still cares about her grandchildren, even as adults. Mother has always claimed that family is what really matters to her. These are the relationships that last, she said.

"Children [are] a reward from [the Lord]" (Ps. 127:3).

We provide security.

Thirteen-year old Margaret flew to Houston alone to visit her grandparents. Following the two-week vacation, she returned home to Connecticut. But when her parents weren't at the gate to meet her plane, she panicked. Margaret ran to the phone and called her grandmother! What should she do, she wondered. Grandma reassured her that her parents were probably delayed in traffic and would be along momentarily.

Sure enough, that's just what happened. But oh, how comforting to know that she could pick up the phone and call Grandma collect during a moment of insecurity. And how nice for grandparents to know their grandchildren can turn to them.

Many young people, however, need their grandparents for much more than a reassuring phone call. Some depend on them for security during a parent's illness or absence, for tender words when they are misunderstood or overlooked at home, for intervention when there is abuse or neglect, or for daily survival if a parent dies or deserts them.

"The Lord is the stronghold of my life"
(Ps. 27:1).

We respect personal boundaries.

When our children grow up, it's difficult to let go of the parenting process as we've known it. It may be even more difficult to refrain from parenting our children's children, especially when we don't approve of our children's parenting style. But conscientious grandparents respect personal boundaries—their own as well as those of their children and grandchildren. They are ready to advise or assist, but they don't push their help. They wait to be invited. Or they offer in a nonmanipulative way that allows the other person to refuse without feeling guilty.

"Whoever loves his brother lives in the light, and there is nothing in him to make him stumble" (1 John 2:10).

We forgive readily.

Most of us can quickly forgive the careless move of a child that results in a spill or a broken vase or a smudge of dirt from muddy sneakers. But what about the deep wounds that result from broken commitments, hurtful words calculated to inflict pain, or neglect and indifference on the part of older grandchildren or their parents?

We can easily be tempted to nurse our grudges, blame our children when our grandchildren hurt and disappoint us, and make the family pay for every little grievance we endure. At times like these, we look to Jesus who carried the burden of all our sin and pain to the cross. As He forgave even the people who treated Him cruelly, He models the forgiveness we can share with our family through God's grace.

"Forgive, and you will be forgiven" (Luke 6:37).

We laugh easily.

Grandparents who forgive readily usually laugh easily as well. Perhaps most important, they can laugh at themselves. They're not afraid to admit their weaknesses and poke a little fun at them. They enjoy the small things—a cute joke, a silly game, a bit of tickling or teasing, the playful antics of a young child, the off-beat humor of a teenager. They see the light instead of the darkness.

"You have filled my heart with greater joy" (Ps. 4:7).

We see the big picture.

While hiking a particularly challenging trail with some friends, a woman stopped in exasperation and exclaimed, "I've had it. We keep going up and down, up and down. We gain 500 feet and then lose 500. This is crazy."

One of the other hikers turned to her and stated calmly, "But overall, we're going up. And the farther up you go, the more of the big picture you see."

What a great reply. Grandparents, more than any other people, have the experience and the maturity to see the big picture; to view life in totality; to know that when the tough times come, they too will pass; to keep in mind that, overall, we're going up.

We can comfort our children and grandchildren in times of crisis, help them gain perspective on a problem by sharing our own experience, lend a hand in a moment of need, and most important, remind them to turn to the Lord for guidance.

I remember my mother often telling me how much she appreciated her father taking us grandkids out for a late afternoon walk so she could get dinner going without interruption.

And another grandfather I spoke with is famous in his family for recounting all the narrow escapes he made during his years as a cross-country trucker. Whenever his children or grandchildren feel overwhelmed by circumstances, he reminds them that if he could "mend" after a broken hip, a coma, and a fractured back, they have nothing to worry about!

"There is a time for everything, and a season for every activity under heaven" (Eccl. 3:1).

We admit our limitations.

It's okay to set limits and acknowledge our limitations. However, some of us find that pretty hard to do. We want to be popular! And we think that if we say "no" or "not now" or "that's a bit too much for me," we might slip down a notch or two. And we might. But so what? I believe our grandkids will respect us for it. And by modeling our humanness, we will be giving our children and grandchildren permission to do the same.

My grandchildren, for example, know that I don't like mass confusion or play without purpose. They also know that I don't climb trees. Mountains, yes. Trees, no!

When we're together, I like to make the time count in a way that includes all of us. We play dress-up or board games, read books together, act out a skit, play tag, or go to the park. (Then we take a rest. That's one of my limits! One the kids don't much like.)

You probably have limits of your own. Some may be physical because of age or a medical condition. Or maybe your personality type is more passive than passionate or more controlling than carefree—and those differences impose limitations. Whatever the reason, I believe it's important for us to know ourselves in this way so we can be fully present to our grandchildren within the boundaries of our own personality and temperament.

"To the man who pleases him, God gives wisdom, knowledge and happiness" (Eccl. 2:26).

We try new experiences.

"I never thought I would play in the dirt," said Grandma Rose. "I don't like dirt under my fingernails, and I don't like inhaling flying dust. Yet there I was, sitting under a big tree, zooming a little car over a dirt trail with my five-year-old grandson. It was a kick! And of course, he thought I was just wonderful."

Other grandparents have confided that a whole new world of experiences opened up to them through their grandchildren.

- hot air ballooning
- picking fresh blueberries and turning them into a pie
- catching a fish too big to reel in alone (by someone who thought she hated fishing till her grandson begged her to come along)
- in-line skating down the beach boardwalk (wearing a helmet and knee pads, of course)
- camping in the desert
- participating in a children's play at church
- finger painting
- compiling a family history for grandchildren
- crawling under and around the furniture after a baby

- traveling halfway around the world to see a newborn grandchild (this account from someone who hates to leave home!)

"The Lord will open ... the storehouse of His bounty" (Deut. 28:12).

Roots and Wings

Grandparents can also provide two essential components for a balanced life: roots and wings. Through us, our grandchildren can discover their history, the origin of the family name, their ancestors, personalities they resemble, or individuals they might like to hear more about.

Grandma and Grandpa can fill in missing details about Great-aunt Mim and distant Uncle Hector. They might know more than just the facts about President Truman for a grandchild who is doing a history report. Perhaps you shook his hand when you were a child.

Maybe an older grandchild is considering joining the Peace Corps or going on a short-term mission with his youth group. You could bring your personal experience to the discussion, if you have lived or served in these capacities, thereby helping both your grandchild and his parents come to a workable decision.

But don't reserve your input just for the serious topics. For example, you may have more in common with your teenage grandchildren than you or they think. Wouldn't it blow their minds to learn that you were an Elvis fan when you were 15? Or that you have a souvenir from a real Beatles concert? Or that you served refreshments when President Ford visited your school? Grandparents provide that vital connection between history that is merely read and history that is lived.

And grandmothers and grandfathers can also provide wings—a blessed and enthusiastic send-off to grandchildren who are ready to strike out on their own. In fact, sometimes parents are not able to do this as easily as grandparents. But grandmothers and grandfathers have been through that stretch of forest before, and they know how important it is to release the fledglings to a solo flight.

Grandparent Heaven

When people ask my husband how he enjoys being a grandparent, his quick reply is: "Heaven is when I'm down on the floor with my grandchildren (nine of them age seven and under) crawling all over me."

You probably have your own viewpoint and definition of grandparent heaven. If not, think about it for a moment. What do you most like about being a grandparent? What do you bring to the role of grandparent? How have your grandchildren blessed you?

If we are to avoid the stereotypes and enjoy our

grandparenting years without guilt and without the imposition of other's standards, it will be important to know who we are and who we are not, what we are willing to do and what we are unwilling to do.

Becoming a "great" grandparent does not merely happen. It requires innovation, commitment and participation as well as a willingness to be the full person God meant us to be—without pretense or apology.

Making Connections

1. List your grandchildren by name and age. Jot down two things about each one that makes that grandchild special to you. Then write down at least two ways you can interact with each one in a personal way. (Examples: water-play with a toddler; ride bikes with a middle-grade child; take a teenager out to dinner and a play or concert, etc.)

2. Put together a photo collage of various stages of your life from childhood to the present. Or combine photos of yourself and other relatives on a family tree. Caption the photos and present to your grandchildren as a gift.

3. Prepare a photo album of pictures of your sons and daughters who have children. Add commentary or captions. Give to your grandchildren.

2

Our Many Names and Faces

Bapa, Grammy, Papa Del, Pippy, Gramps, Grams, Grandmom, Granddad, Gramama, Grampy, Grandmaw, Grandpaw, Gramma, Grampa, Paw-Paw, Gah-paw, Nana, Papa, Grandmother, Grandfather ... and the list goes on. The most popular names on the role call, however, are still Grandma and Grandpa. But even though many of us share the same "name," we are as different in color and texture and design and shape as a patchwork quilt.

Some of us are retired. Others are active in our lifework. Still others have taken on the challenge of raising grandchildren in the absence of their parents.

Bonnie and Warren (Grandma and Grandpa to six-year-old Andrew and three-year-old Lindsey) live in a townhouse and operate a home-based consulting business. They're active on the tennis court as well as in their church, and they enjoy playing with their grandchildren, taking walks, building sand castles on the beach, and baking cookies.

In fact, Andrew loves Grandma's peanut-butter cookies so much, he's memorized the recipe: "First you make brown dough. You take a little bit and roll it in a ball. Then you roll it in a snake. You put it on the pan and smash it with a fork and then bake it. Then you can eat it."

Granny L. is a homemaker, and her husband is a stockbroker. They've lived in the same home and belonged to the same church for 32 years. Though their grandson Kirby is not quite two and little Nicole is just under a year, Granny L. is already building a bond with each one of them. She writes letters to Kirby, who lives about six hours away, and visits Nicole in person because she is only 20 minutes away by car.

Granny L. even learned to do some simple graphics on the computer so she can decorate her letters to Kirby. A popular one, I'm sure, is a cute little teddy bear.

Suzanne and Ed Ray are grandparents of 10 grandchildren ranging in age from two to 13. Gramma says, "I think they enjoy the undivided, loving attention and the gentle playfulness we share."

Grampa (Paw-Paw to some of the children) says, "The most important thing is to do ordinary things together regularly."

He encourages the children to help him pick oranges, work with him in the garage, clean the fire pit, etc. The Rays also play board games, work puzzles, and enjoy bicycling and boogie boarding with their grandchildren. Both are retired so they also have time to travel extensively, hike, swim, backpack, and camp.

After special times together, Suzanne likes to reminisce on the phone or in letters. "I remind them in little ways of our happy times together. For example, I might tell my 11-year-old grandson that when I went on a mule pack trip, I used the Boy Scout knots he taught me. Or I might tell another one that I still have the pretty shells we gathered together on the beach."

To Henry and Betty Shimozono, on the other hand, grandparenting is a brand-new role, one they are already enjoying even though little Alexander is only two months old and lives a couple of thousand miles away. But they will meet him and get to hold him for the first time during a Christmas visit.

"We don't know what name he will call us," said Grandmother Betty, "but *his* middle name, Mitsuo, has tremendous significance. He was named after the lead pilot of 360 planes who bombed Pearl Harbor on December 7, 1941.

"Following the war, however, Captain Mitsuo Fuchida became a Christian and then an evangelist. Our entire family had the privilege of meeting him in Japan, where he retired during the 1970s.

"After our son Mark remembered this remark-able warrior, and named his son after him, he discovered that little Alexander Mitsuo's birthday, September 2, 1994, was the 49th anniversary of the signing of the peace treaty that ended World War II. So to us, this grandchild is a peace child!"

Both Henry and Betty are still employed, Betty as a medical technologist and Henry as a chaplain for the Veteran's Administration Medical Center in San Diego. They are both active in their home church, visiting those in need in hospitals and homes, and praying for their pastor and others as members of the prayer team.

Dave and Elaine have three grandchildren, one a teenager and two under three years of age. The older one, Helen, lives nearby, but the little ones, Amy and Alex, left Northern California for the Eastern Mediterranean in early 1995. Their parents are missionaries for Wycliffe Bible Translators.

Both Dave and Elaine are still working in their professions as maintenance control supervisor and software engineer. Dave enjoys flying, and Elaine loves to read. They are also planning and saving for the time they can build a new house on some property they own in Southern California.

Elaine and Dave don't see their grandchildren often because of the distance. While they haven't had the opportunity some grandparents have to build a close relationship, they are contributing in ways that are meaningful to them. For example, Elaine said they purchased a mint set of American coins for both Amy and Alex the year of their births. "I'd like to do the same for any future grandchildren we may have," Elaine added.

The McDonalds are retired. Kathy was a travel agent until last year, and Bill was in the banking industry. They have five grandchildren and see four of them at least a couple of times a month.

"Our daughter says we make things fun for the children. They like our spontaneity," said Kathy. Dancing in the living room, eating on trays that are just for children, reading books, watching movies, and going on special outings are all part of the fun the children anticipate with a trip to Pa Pa's and Pippy's, names the children made up and that have stuck!

Bill loves to play sports with the children, and Kathy enjoys gardening with them. They both dream of taking them all on a family vacation to a dude ranch, Mexico, or Hawaii. But then Kathy admits, "The kids would have to be older, and we'd have to be richer!"

The McDonalds are active in their church, hosting a weekly home fellowship group. Bill also serves as an elder and Kathy as a volunteer in the church office.

"We pray with the children, and we give thanks a lot!" said Kathy. "I believe they see us as Christian grandparents who love Jesus and who love them."

Some grandparents I spoke with are also great-grandparents. Edith D. is one. She has two grown grandchildren and one great-granddaughter born this year.

"Both grandchildren call us Grandma and Grandpa," said Edith, an 84-year-old housewife who is still married to her husband of 57 years. She enjoys reading, sewing, and writing letters. Her husband is an avid bridge player and reader, walks every day, and keeps his thumb on the pulse of finance. Edith's greatest joy is serving the Lord and encouraging people.

At this time in her life, Edith says she is content to be at home. Their travel days are over, though when her husband was in business, she and their children joined him on several trips to different parts of the world.

"Today I volunteer in a nursing home, head a prayer chain in our church, and volunteer in the church office," Edith said.

Quimby and Mabel Duntley are also in their 80s and retired. He worked as a scientist, and she was a homemaker and earlier, a musician. Today they enjoy taking Bible classes and, as Mabel puts it, "digging into the Scriptures."

All the grandchildren have always called them Grandma and Grandpa, but Mabel and Quimby also have been baby-sitter, playmate, and friend. "We like to think we were influential in their lives as a teacher. And we're very happy that they seek us out as helpmates and confidantes as well," Mabel said.

Mabel said she and Quimby have tried to enrich their grandchildren's lives spiritually and culturally, by "teaching them Christian ideals and the Bible. We've also taken them on trips, and the older ones remember interesting details about their grandfather's career involving fascinating projects, inventions, and developments for our government during World War II."

Some grandparents travel the world. Some live on a quiet street in a small town. Others live on a houseboat and come to shore only on weekends. Still others live with their children and grandchildren and help run the extended household.

Some grandparents are as young as 37 or as old as 96 ... or older! Some are active. Some are passive. Some are ill. Others are well and able and eager to be part of the lives of their grandchildren of any age. Some like to play. Others like to observe. Some like to travel. Some like to stay home.

But whatever the name or the face or the personality or the profession or the status, all the grandparents I talked with have one unmistakable characteristic in common—a deep and abiding love for their grandchildren and for their Lord.

And what do they most want to be remembered for?

I want them to remember how much I loved Jesus and how much I loved them.
                              Grandma Julie

That we were always there for them if needed. We loved them. And to put Jesus first in their hearts.
            Grandma Mabel and Grandpa Quimby

To remember that Grandma prayed for them daily, that God is watching over them and protecting them, and that He loves them unconditionally, just as they are. And that Grandpa loved them too—in his own quiet way.
                              Grandma Edith

That I loved the Lord, cared for their moms and dads, was crazy about them, and was FUN!
                                  Pippy

I hope my grandchildren will remember me as someone who loved them dearly and loved the Lord with all my heart.
                            Grandmaw Elaine

I want my grandchildren to remember that first and foremost in my life is the Lord, that I really loved them, and that I was a man of honesty.
                                    Grandpa Charles

*I hope they remember that no matter what, we were there for them, **always**.*
                                    Grandma Joanie

I would like to be remembered as a woman of prayer. I have prayed daily for my grandchild from the time I knew he had been conceived. I want him to remember me as a grandmother who shared her personal testimony with him along with spiritual milestones in my life and as a person who modeled a life of simplicity, contentment, and growing old with grace.
                                    Grandma Betty

I would like our grandchildren to remember that we loved the Lord, and we loved them.
                                    Grandpa Henry

I want to be remembered as a positive example of Christian love and a good and positive example of growing old.
                                    Granny L.

Most important, I would like them to remember me for my faith in God, which I want to share with them, and as someone who really loved and cared for them. They are very special to me.
Grandma Bonnie

Making Connections

1. What name do your grandchildren call you? Maybe you have more than one. Spend a few moments writing down what that name (or names) means to you and what being a grandparent signifies in your life.

2. Write an original "grandparent's prayer." Make it as personal to you and your grandchildren as you can. Include that prayer in your daily prayer time. You might even wish to send copies to your grandchildren.

3. Write down three things you would most like your grandchildren to remember about you. What can you do now to make that a reality?

3

A LIFE OF YOUR OWN

Ginny looked up from her chicken salad in the hotel cafe where we had stopped for lunch. She thumbed through the photos of my grandchildren, then handed them back.

"I have to admit, I'm jealous," she said, turning her gaze in my direction. "Being a grandmother sounds like such fun and so fulfilling. But I wonder if I'll ever get the chance. I drop hints every once in awhile, but Don and Cara said they're not ready. And with her health problems, I'm not sure they ever will be. I hate the thought of living the rest of my life without holding a grandbaby."

I could appreciate Ginny's feelings. She had experienced a series of losses in her life, the death of her husband when her son Don was only three years old, then her mother from cancer, and more recently, a niece she had "mothered" had gone off to college. Ginny longed for another young person to focus on and love. She was a giver through and through.

On another occasion, Anita, a grandmother of four, shared her perspective. "I can't imagine not seeing my grandchildren every day," she said. Anita lives next door to them. "They make my life worthwhile. If I didn't have the kids and my daughter to think about, I'm not sure what I'd do at this stage of my life."

I met her daughter and was surprised at how well this arrangement seems to work for her too. She said her mother has been such a part of her family, she doesn't think she could manage without her.

Ginny's and Anita's are two very different situations, but I noticed one remarkable similarity. Both women seemed to believe their lives wouldn't be valuable or satisfying without grandchildren. One mourns the fact that she doesn't have any and focuses on that. The other focuses on the grandchildren she has and can't move beyond them.

Quite a different scenario involves Marion and Jan. They're both grandmothers in their early 50s, and they are also a writing team. They write children's books and participate in author fairs at schools and libraries around their state.

"My grandkids are so proud of me," said Marion. "They love to show their friends my books in the library. It's a kick for me. I've spoken at both their schools. But they know that writing isn't just a game. I have to spend regular hours at my desk. Jan does too. We love being grandparents, but we also have a life apart from being grandmothers. I think it's healthy. I can't live for someone else. I have to be a person in my own right."

Jan agrees. She said that realization came to her recently when a friend of hers shared the tearful news that her son and daughter-in-law and their children were moving abroad for a year.

"My friend was so devastated, it really stopped me. It made me think about how I'd react if my grandchildren moved away," said Jan. "I must admit, I didn't like the feeling. I felt the loss just thinking about it. But then I thought about the other parts of my life and I relaxed. I have my husband, my church friends, my partner Marion, and my work as a writer.

"These are very satisfying relationships and experiences," Jan added, fingering the jacket of one of her books. "I'd miss the children, of course, and I'd want to keep in close contact with them, but I don't think I'd be devastated. I wouldn't want to think that the loss of anything or anyone would really devastate me. I have the Lord, and I have the life He gave me. That matters more than anything."

Still other grandparents have a hard time staying involved with their grandchildren. They don't like the noise and the chaos that seems to go with little children. Or they're still busy with their careers. Traditionally, this has been more true of men, but with so many women working today, grandmothers, too, are feeling the stress of trying to do it all.

"I love 'em to pieces," said one grandmother about her three grandchildren. "But I'm exhausted at the end of my week, and I don't have much energy left for wiggly little kids."

She sees them, of course, but she said that until she retires, her time is limited. "I feel a little guilty about that," she said. "Many of my friends spend much more time with their grandkids than I do."

I was happy to discover that many men enjoy a thriving relationship with their grandchildren. A woman I met this summer said her husband was taking care of their daughter's children for the weekend while the daughter was in a surfing contest! And where was Grandma? In the mountains with me and 13 other women on an all-women's mule pack trip!

This grandfather had no problem jumping right into the middle of whatever was going on in order to free up his daughter and son-in-law. How great!

Not Guilty!

According to my informal survey, some grandparents feel guilty if they don't have a life of their own—because they think they should. Others feel guilty if they do have a life they enjoy and, as a result, don't spend as much time as they'd like with their grandchildren. Either way, it's a no-win situation that produces guilt and self-judgment.

I feel certain of one thing. *It's okay, in fact it's*

important and necessary, for each of us to have a life apart from grandparenting. We need definition and purpose beyond our role in the life of our children and grand-children. We were on earth before them, and they are likely to be here long after we're gone, so it's not healthy to cling to them for our identity.

Root Causes

If you struggle with your role as grandparent, giving away too much of yourself because of your need to be needed, or backing off for fear of being consumed by your children or grandchildren, or because you are busy with your career or other com-mitments, you may want to look at the possible roots of your beliefs and behavior. Either way you are not free to be yourself—a grandparent and a person without guilt. Perhaps you can identify with some of the causes listed below, compiled from comments shared by a variety of grandparents. You may realize, as they did, that your feelings of inadequacy or guilt or resistance may stem from your own childhood.

You grew up in an emotionally distant family.

You did not see honest and open displays of affection, approval, or acceptance. Nor did you see anyone model true grief or anger or sadness. As you grew up in this climate, you probably soon discovered that no one could handle your strong emotions either. If you did express yourself honestly, you were told to "cool it" or to "be more considerate of others." You began to believe that you didn't count. What others wanted of you was more important than what you wanted for yourself.

A child who comes from such an environment is very likely to live his or her entire life trying to be someone other than who he or she is. And that behavior will carry over to our grandparenting experiences because the older we get, the more our fears intensify if we are not aware of them. We abandon ourselves further as we cling more and more to our families, seeking identity and refuge in our role as parents of adult children and as grandparents. Or our response may be to push them away or hang back because we cannot handle the intimacy involved.

You learned to control other people by expressing your dependence on them.

You may have been taught that the only way to hold onto others—and thus your own life—was to be dependent on those close to you, first parents, then children, and finally grandchildren. At this point in your life, you might welcome some time to yourself, some quiet and peace, a hobby or part-time job that would be just for you, but you feel ill-equipped to do any of these things because you're not convinced you can—or should. Children who grow up depending on others for their happiness and fulfillment are never truly happy or fulfilled. No one can do that for us. Your relationship with your grandchildren, then, will not be authentic, rather it will be a dependency that stems from the lack in your own childhood.

> *You accepted the message that you weren't important enough to develop your full potential as a person.*

I think this is a chronic state for many people in our culture. They don't know who they are. And this is not only true of non-Christians. Many believers live out their lives under the same dark cloud. They don't know who they are in Christ. And they don't know their place in the world. They have not been encouraged or taught to believe that they are valuable just because of who they are. So they create value by performing or doing for their children and grandchildren. Such men and women need permission to explore their own identity and to discover aspects of life that are not dependent on what other people think.

> *You feel worthy only when you spend time, energy, and money on your children and grandchildren.*

If you grew up in a home where your mother was a full-time caregiver, then your sense of worth may depend on how much you do for your family and others and how little you do for yourself. Even if you work outside your home, you may feel compelled to use your earnings to support part of your children's lifestyle or to pay tuition or clothing needs for your grandchildren. You provide the birthday parties for your grandson and granddaughter or the dance lessons or the summer camp fees—even if it means going without something necessary in your own life, such as basic medical care or saving for your old age. Devoting yourself to your family in this way makes you feel good about yourself. You may even notice that you *have* to do it.

You live in a state of longing.

Grandparents who live *through* others are not only a burden to others but to themselves because no other person can fulfill them. They find themselves living in a constant state of desire, never quite sure what it is they want or need but feeling irritable and discontent.

Perhaps as a child you were continually denied even the most basic desires. If you asked for a bicycle like other kids had, you were told there was no money for that. If you wanted to purchase a special book or attend an event or participate in a sport, you may have been ridiculed or dismissed for whatever reason.

So you grew up with a deep hunger that was never satisfied. As an adult, you may still experience these feelings, even if you have a loving family and darling grandchildren all around you. If you recognize these feelings within yourself, it may be time to open up to your needs and wants and to give yourself some of the pleasures you were denied as a child.

Have you always longed to write or paint or act? One grandfather I know participates in community theater twice a year. Another is an "extra" in the San Diego Opera. A 65-year-old grandmother I read about in the newspaper just had her second book published to good reviews. She didn't even start writing seriously until she was 60.

Men and women who seek fulfillment for themselves find they enjoy their children and grandchildren even more. They no longer make their family their only focus but include them as part of their larger life. They also notice that their families are more interested in them when they bring something new and stimulating to the relationships.

You feel that life is passing you by.

I've heard it said there are four kinds of people in the world: those who organize the parade, those who march in it, those who stand on the sidelines and watch it, and those who say, "What parade?"

Where do you fit? If you are one who is hanging

on the sidelines as others step out and pass you, you may feel very angry inside. You may even feel competitive with your young grandchildren as they move into the world and claim their spot, going to school, learning about computers, experiencing sports and the arts, etc. Maybe you were denied these opportunities when you were growing up, and now, watching them, you're reminded of how shallow your life has become.

But it's never too late to join the parade. In fact, many grandparents claim it is their grandchildren who have inspired them to march! There are now many groups and clubs in churches and communities throughout the country specifically geared to adults who want to learn new skills, take up a hobby, or volunteer their time and talent. No one needs to stand on the sidelines—unless they choose to.

Making Connections

1. Consider the root causes of resistance to intimacy, guilt regarding the time you spend with grandchildren, or a tendency to over-focus on them. Do you relate to any of them? Would you like to change your behavior? If so, in what way?

2. What have you been putting off that you would

like to experience? What steps could you take to make this a reality?

3. How do you think nurturing yourself could also nurture your grandchildren and their parents? Give some specific examples.

4

MORE THAN A BABY-SITTER

*"I love taking care of my grandkids once in
awhile, but sometimes I feel as though that's all
my children want from me."*

*"I take care of my grandchildren while my son
and daughter-in-law work. I'd rather baby-sit
them than see someone else do it."*

*"My kids call me first when they need a sitter. I
want them to. I can't always say yes, but I do
whenever I can."*

I've heard these and other comments from many
grandfathers and grandmothers. Inevitably, the topic
of baby-sitting came into the conversation—sometimes in a critical yet playful way: "Oh, I'm the usual
baby-sitter, I guess, though I'm not sure I like it. After
all, I raised my own kids. Let them raise theirs.
(Smile.)"

Grandparents also talked about how busy their
children and grandchildren were. There's never
enough time to really be together.

"Baby-sitting is about the only time I spend any quality time with my grandson," said one man. I wondered whose fault that was. Maybe he needed to be encouraged to take his grandson on some outings or invite him over to his house to do some gardening or to work in his photography lab. I would imagine his grandson would have loved to learn these skills from his granddad.

Many grandparents I spoke with said they enjoyed helping their sons and daughters with baby-sitting. Some didn't mind once in awhile, but they didn't want to make it a habit. Others baby-sat occasionally and/or reluctantly. Still others baby-sit full time while parents work.

Beyond Baby-Sitting

Being a grandparent, however, doesn't go hand-in-hand with baby-sitting. If you're one who can't or won't, don't feel guilty. As helpful as it is to young parents to have grandma or grandpa baby-sit once in awhile, I believe they appreciate us even more when we contribute to our grandchildren in ways that go beyond baby-sitting.

For example, Judy W. shared that her father was a gifted teacher, particularly in mathematics. "He wasn't much for changing diapers or playing games, but he made such an impression on my daughter with his ability to teach. She has his talent, and now she's a math major at the University of Minnesota and plans to become a math professor. I think she'll always be grateful to Papa for the time he spent with her on math and science projects."

William S. remembers his grandmother for the music she brought into his life. "I was an only child," he said, "and Nana lived with my parents and me, so I was exposed to classical music at a very young age.

"She took me to outdoor concerts in the park during the summer when I was small," William explained. "As I got older, she bought season tickets to a Mozart Festival each year for the two of us. I can't remember a time when I didn't want to be a violinist like Nana."

"My grandmother had a wonderful ability to listen," said Rosemary, now a grandmother herself. "I could go to her anytime, about anything, and she would make time for me. I honestly believe she had more to do with shaping my self-image than my parents.

"And whether I shared something funny or frightening, she'd always close the conversation with the same sentence, 'Now let's give that to the Lord and trust Him for the perfect answer.' I miss her to this day," said Rosemary with tears in her eyes. "I hope I can be the kind of grandmother to little Carol that Grandma Lois was to me."

Ron said his grandfather was his hockey coach as a kid. "When I was seven, my dad died. My grandfather moved in with Mom and me after that. He thought getting involved in a sport would help me through the tough times. Since he had played hockey as a kid, he suggested I sign up for a hockey team.

"Then he volunteered to be one of the coaches, and I was ecstatic. Hockey became our thing," Ron said. "I'll always remember my grandfather for the way he entered into my life when I really needed a father figure."

Missed Opportunities

On the other hand, there are grandparents who miss precious opportunities to share their talent and wisdom with their grandchildren.

Angelica, a 66-year-old grandmother from Italy, lives with her son and his family. Italian is her native tongue, yet neither of her son's children speak the language. What a loss—for her and for the boys. Angelica said she put the old country behind her when she moved here. "What do they need Italian for? They live in America!" she said.

Angelica has contributed to her son's family by cooking, cleaning, and baby-sitting. She does not see herself in any capacity beyond these activities. But here is a woman of enormous inner courage and conviction, with stories and personal experiences of danger and persecution and loss that would inspire anyone who listens.

Kent's father discounts his skill. "This man was a master with wood," said Kent. "He built the house I was raised in and provided for my mom and us six kids as a carpenter and furniture finisher.

"But my boys hardly know anything about this side of him," Kent added. "He seems to be embarrassed when I bring it up. He says he hopes they'll do something with their minds, not their hands."

I believe there are thousands of grandparents all across the United States, who, like Angelica and Kent's dad, overlook the opportunities they have to reach out to their grandchildren, to influence and inspire them in ways they've never considered.

This truth came home to me while visiting my grandchildren. One morning as we set out for the neighborhood park, I saw a woman on the front sidewalk, pushing a stroller with a toddler in the seat and a boy of about seven or eight walking alongside her. My grandchildren introduced the boy to me as their friend Mark and then acknowledged his grandma and little sister.

"We're on the way to park," I said. "Can the children come along?"

"Oh no," she said. "I baby-sit while their parents work. I can't let them out of my sight."

"Would you like to come too?" I asked.

She thought about it for a moment, then launched into a litany of all the things she had to do each week to keep her son's house in order and to take care of the children and the many problems she had with her health. "At the end of the day," she admitted, "I'm exhausted."

But she decided to walk to the park with us anyway. As we continued talking, I could tell this woman took her role as baby-sitter very seriously.

Along the way, my grandchildren and I stopped at a favorite climbing tree where Noah likes to stretch his limbs (and the tree limbs too). Quickly he scrambled up the trunk and perched on a heavy branch.

Mark followed, a bit reserved, but still having fun. Next, my grandson Jacob reminded me that this is the spot where we play our make-believe game Witch, something we created after reading a library book.

I got down on my hands and knees and suddenly, in the middle of our playacting, I realized the other grandmother was looking at me absolutely wide-eyed. I think she thought I had lost it! But Jacob and Johannah and I were having such fun, I didn't want to cut it short. At the end of the game, I got up, dusted off my hands, and off we went to the park.

After swinging and sliding till we were out of breath, we played another favorite make-believe game, Fire Fighter/911. Once again the woman looked at me as if I needed emergency treatment!

She watched a bit longer, then excused herself, saying it was time to make lunch. Not once during our entire time together did she speak to the children or play with them. The little girl stayed in the stroller most of the time, except for a few minutes on the swing.

I knew this caring grandmother loved those kids fiercely. She held and kissed the toddler and soothed her when she was fussy. She protected them intently, watching the street as they crossed, and making certain to keep her eyes on them at all times. But she was so serious that I wondered if she and her grandchildren weren't missing out on just being together.

I made this mistake as a mother when my children were young. I was so busy doing what I thought was correct and right that I was not as emotionally present as I wish I had been. My children are still learning things about me that they never knew—because I didn't realize then how vital to their identity certain knowledge about me, their mother, would be.

I don't want that to happen in my relationship with my grandchildren. I want them to know who I am—weaknesses as well as strengths. And I want to know all about them.

I believe that many grandparents resist or apologize for the unique and wonderful perspective and talent they could bring to their role as grandparents because they don't recognize their importance. They don't think they matter. Instead, they retreat into behavior most commonly associated with grandparents—baby-sitting. Or they hang back, willing to live on the periphery of their grandchildren's lives instead of being part of the center.

Some grandparents remain on the edge not because they can't extend themselves but because they don't know how to get involved, or they don't know that it would matter if they did. They don't realize that *who they are* does matter. That *who they are* does make a difference. That *who they are* is a gift in so many more ways than they might believe.

Now is the time to begin participating in more active and meaningful ways. If you are already doing that, then you know what it is to pass on wisdom and knowledge and experience so that your grandchildren's lives will be enriched and deepened.

If you're not involved in a personal way and you want to be, spend some time looking into your life and the lives of your grandchildren. How can you create a bridge between you? What could you do or share that would help them know you on a deeper level? What would you like to know about them? How could you contribute in a way that will draw them out and help them grow as individuals? Here are some things to consider.

Be a playmate.

Young children are thrilled when you sit on the floor with them and roll a ball back and forth, or crawl in and around the furniture, or turn out the lights and play hide-and-seek. I am amazed at how these simple, traditional games continue to delight boys and girls. The more physical you can be with them, the more they like it.

In my oldest daughter's household, every night after dinner the three older kids (ages three through seven) rush to the family bed with their dad. They roughhouse until everyone is either worn out or crying because they didn't get enough!

Yesterday, while listening to a radio show on parenting, the host, a Christian marriage and family counselor, made the point that wrestling with your kids is an important component of good parenting. And dads shouldn't be afraid to be physical with their younger daughters in this way, he said. They, too, need to become comfortable with their bodies and their ability to use them in play.

I was reminded then of how my father played with my children. They thought he was "the best" grandpa in the whole world. Whenever we visited, there was always at least one wrestling event or a game of hide-and-seek under the big quilt on his and my mother's bed. The kids would squeal and squirm as Grandpa chased and tickled them.

During summer visits, he would carry on in the swimming pool in the same way, chasing after them to their delight, wearing an old, beat-up hat to keep the sun off his face. They playfully regarded him as a "left-over lifeguard!" What memories they have.

My husband now carries on that tradition in our family with his three grandsons. Almost the minute we have our feet in the door, Charles is on the floor. He's a make-shift horse, pony, or train, wiggling in and out of furniture, down the halls and around the corners with three tiny passengers whooping and hollering for him to keep going (while I pray silently that he doesn't drop over from heart failure)!

I realize this kind of strong play will not feel comfortable (or be physically possible) for every grandparent. But it's an example of how much children love it when adults, especially grandparents, interact with them on their level.

My mother was great about playing jump rope, jacks, or checkers with my children, and she was willing to get down on the floor to color or paste or play a board game. I'm carrying on her tradition with my grandchildren. I'm not into roughhousing, but I love crafts and games and playacting.

The important thing is to be genuine. Look at yourself as realistically as you can, and then choose the kind of play you can and will enter into with enthusiasm. Offer that to your grandkids. Have some alternatives ready. For example:

> *"I don't like playing tag, but I'd love to color with you or play with your train."*

> *"I'd like to get some fresh air. Let's save the card game for later. How about a game of catch?"*

Bonnie shared that she'll play board games with her grandson and granddaughter, but it's not her favorite thing to do. On the other hand, she loves to cook with them and to share her recipe for making bubbles! Six-year-old Andrew likes that too.

Mostly, our grandkids just want to be with us. They're usually willing to compromise if we are.

Be a pal.

Many grandchildren think of their grandmas and grandpas as pals—a fun person to hang out with at the lake, fishing or swimming; in the den, watching football or working a puzzle; on a hill, gazing at the trees or hiking through the woods.

Your grandkids also can pal around with you as you run errands. One grandfather said he and his grandson have their best talks when they're driving. "He just opens up," said Grandpa John. "I don't have to do much but listen. Sometimes he wants my opinion about something, and I'm happy to give it."

"I love taking her out for walks in the stroller and just talking to her," said one young grandmother of her seven-month-old granddaughter. "We walk down to the ocean near her home and I point out the waves and the rocks, and we look at the seals. I hope we'll always be able to spend time together like this. She's my 'little pal.' "

What a great beginning for a relationship between grandma and granddaughter. If they are pals now, chances are they always will be.

Be a friend.

In San Diego, one of the local television stations, Channel 10, sponsors a community-wide program called "Ten Friends," which brings together school-age children and the elderly. Whenever I see clips of the program, I am inspired by the devotion the children exhibit for the men and women they meet. It's not uncommon to see a boy or girl playing a game, coloring a picture, or building something with one of the elderly men and women.

"We're good friends," says one little girl with her arm around an adopted grandmother.

"We have fun together," says a boy in the midst of a game with an elderly companion.

Children, more than anyone, seem to understand the nature and value of friendship. Friends from their peer group are important to them, of course. But they also desire adult friends in their lives. And what better friend could a child have than a trusted grandparent?

The Thorndike Barnhart Dictionary defines the word friend as "a person who knows and likes another; a chum, crony, companion; a person who favors and supports."

As a friend to your grandchildren, you are one who "knows and likes" them. And as your friend, they know and like you. Notice, the definition does not qualify. The phrase "knows and likes" is inclusive, embracing all parts of the individual, both the strengths and the weaknesses. How much we all need this kind of "favor and support," regardless of our age.

And who could give it more freely than children and grandparents?

Children, still learning and growing and feeling their way in life, need someone to stand by them and affirm and forgive them. And they are naturally more compassionate than most adults.

Grandparents, at their stage of life, are generally more able to offer this encouragement and compassion than adults of a younger age. They have lived long enough to understand the growing-up process. And they also treasure the love and loyalty of their young grandchildren who often see them as heros.

Be a spiritual model.

As Christians, we have a unique opportunity to share our faith with our grandchildren, to share our love of Jesus, and to help them build their relationship with the Lord. How comforting it is for a child to look to a grandparent for spiritual modeling. Even if a child has devoted Christian parents, children need and want to know that their grandma and grandpa also know the Lord and trust Him.

You can enrich your grandchildren's spiritual journey by reading with them, listening to Christian music and tapes especially for kids, and attending Christian programs, retreats, and youth events. Edith said one of her warm memories of time spent with her two grandchildren, who are now grown, is reading Bible stories together.

Depending on your schedule, you might even participate as a helper or volunteer at an event for children or teens such as an Advent workshop, vacation Bible school, youth camp, etc. Imagine the impact you would make on their spiritual lives through something so simple, yet selfless.

Having a strong and certain walk with the Lord yourself is, of course, the most important way to model the Christian experience. If your grandchildren see you pray, they are likely to pray too. If they see you attend church, they go. If they see you go to God with your problems and worries, they are going to go to Him as well. If they hear you confess wrong-doing and ask their forgiveness and God's, they will happily experience God's forgiveness and unconditional love in Jesus and learn to share it with others.

Dianna said she wants to be remembered for the times she and her granddaughter Alexis prayed together and talked about Jesus. What a special legacy.

Be an advisor.

Teenage and young adult grandchildren often turn to their grandparents as advisors, especially when they are dealing with some of life's tough issues. A grandmother or grandfather can be an invaluable source of strength and support during a personal trial, such as a divorce in their family, or the death of a parent or school friend.

Young people also value the advice of grandparents when they are considering their choices about college, relocating, a job search, or a marriage partner. Some grandparents may resist their importance at such times. But the young people I've spoken with quickly proved to me that the difference in age or geographic distance didn't lessen their need for their grandparents' wisdom and support.

"When I broke up with my boyfriend last year," said Laurie, "I called my grandma right away. She really liked Jay, and I knew she'd understand how I felt. And she did. She also told me that she and Grandpa would be praying for me.

"Then she shared something with me I never knew before," Laurie continued. "She and Grandpa had broken up before they got married. The invitations were in the mail and Grandma had her dress and shoes and everything. It nearly killed her, she said.

"But then she took it to the Lord," Laurie said. "She realized that she had made Grandpa more important in her life than God. That scared her because she had always thought she loved God more than anyone. She made a new commitment to Jesus that day, to always put Him first. Then she let go of Grandpa in her heart, even though it was really hard.

"Six weeks later he came back and proposed to her," Laurie said with a smile. "He said he knew she was the girl for him. And all her feelings came back too."

Laurie was beaming as she related this story. She said it really made her think about her priorities. Maybe, like her grandmother, she had put Jay ahead of the Lord. "I need to take a good look at that," she said.

Imagine the contribution this grandmother made to her granddaughter's life. It sounded life-changing to me—a life-changing impact only a grandparent could have made.

Mabel and Quimby are delighted when their

grown grandchildren ask for advice and encouragement. "What would you do in this situation?" or "How did you handle this or that when you were my age?" are familiar questions that indicate Mabel and Quimby's opinions and experiences are valuable, no matter what their age.

Be a teacher.

Grandparents are among a child's first teachers. My grandfather taught me about my Irish roots, how to play checkers, tips on bowling, and how to laugh and not take life too seriously.

Any grandparent can be a teacher. No degree or license is required—just a willing heart and an eager grandchild. Parents, of course, are a child's primary teachers, but grandmothers and grandfathers run a close second. Generally, they are more patient and less serious as teachers than parents are. Grandparents have been around for awhile. They have a wider view of life and can exercise the right amount of comfort and encouragement.

They can teach their grandchildren about photography, cooking, gardening, painting, music, or sports, or they can teach by example and conversation and application. For example, as your grandchild helps you plant and nurture and harvest a garden, he or she will learn by doing. If you play tennis with your grandchildren, it's a fine time to help them improve their serve or rush the net. If you want to teach them about the Lord, there's no better way than to read Bible stories and pray together out loud.

Don't underestimate your ability to teach. Actually, grandparents teach whether or not they intend to. Ask any grandchild!

Be a confidante.

"I can tell my grandmother anything," said 17-year-old Michael. "Even if I was doing drugs, I think I could tell her, and she'd help me find a way out."

What a tribute! How blessed Michael is to have such a grandmother. And what a privilege it is to have that kind of relationship with a grandson.

Children and teens live in a very troubled world. They not only need solid friends of all age groups in their lives, they also need at least one true confidante—someone they can be completely real with, a person who can handle the truth about them without freaking out. The child who has a grandparent for a confidante is blessed indeed.

Think about your grandchildren. Do they feel safe around you? Could they tell you anything and trust that you wouldn't run away? Could they count on you to provide stability and strength during a crisis? It may be that you'll never have to accept this much responsibility, but it's something to consider before it happens.

Edith says she most enjoys being a confidante to her grandchildren, as well as a friend and encourager. "When they were small, I had much fun playing with them, reading Bible stories, trying to teach my granddaughter to sew, cooking their favorite foods, and taking them to the beach and the zoo."

Being a grandparent is a lot more than being a baby-sitter. But don't discount the value of being that too. The best grandparent is one who can be a pal, a playmate, a friend, a spiritual model, an advisor, a teacher, or a confidante—and a baby-sitter too!

Making Connections

1. What new insight about your role as grandparent did you gain from this chapter? How might you apply what you learned to your life?

2. What new aspect of your grandparenting role would you like to explore (playmate, pal, teacher, spiritual model, etc.)? What practical steps could you take to put this into action?

3. Based on what you read in this chapter, write down three ways you could foster more intimacy/closeness between you and your grandchildren.

PART 2

MEMORIES ARE
MADE OF THIS

5

MAKING
MEMORIES/
BUILDING
TRADITIONS

In Minneapolis, four-year-old Katie is helping her Granny Julia make colorful paper chains for the Christmas tree. Granny patiently shows her where to put the glue on the cut strips and how to link one paper loop through another. As they work, Granny explains that when she was a girl in the 1940s, she made the same kind of Christmas tree chains with her grandmother. "In fact," she says, "there may even be a piece of one left in my treasure box."

In a beach community in Southern California, 12-year-old Richard is taking a few pointers from his 60-year-old grandfather, who is getting ready for a senior surfing contest! "He's really cool to watch," said Richard, obviously proud to have such a contemporary grandfather.

In Berea, Kentucky, an 18-year-old young man tours the campus of Berea College with his grandmother, a 1945 graduate of the college. He's the third generation to attend the school. He hopes to join the family retail business after graduation.

Similar events occur every day in the lives of thousands of grandparents and grandchildren throughout the world. The younger generation learns from the older generation or follows their path in some way. And the grandparents are rejuvenated by the energy and enthusiasm of their grandchildren and proud to share what they know—whether it's their experience or expertise.

Memories are made of all these things.

Memory-Makers

I think of grandparents as memory-makers. Certainly children and parents create memories together, but the ones grandparents create are unique. Grandparents provide maturity, life experience and wisdom, enriching their grandchildren's lives in a way no one else can.

Consider some of the ways you can make memories and build traditions with your grandchildren.

Share quality time together. It will multiply.

Find out what each grandchild likes to do and build that activity or event into your routine together. For example, whenever my grandson Noah comes to San Diego, he wants to climb the hills by the ocean—

a "range" he refers to as Magah's Mountains. Then we walk out to the end of Crystal Pier and watch people fish and surf.

Two-and-a-half-year-old Jacob, on the other hand, likes playing Witch with me in the dirt under a big climbing tree. Johannah loves it when I polish her nails or let her borrow my lipstick and eye shadow.

All three love a good game of Freeze Tag in the vacant lot near their home. These activities are as much a part of our routine together as eating dinner or brushing our teeth before bed. I doubt that any of us will ever forget these simple traditions. The best part is we didn't "work" at them. They have simply emerged. And because we have so much fun, we repeat them whenever we're together.

Share a little money.
It will come back to you.

Most young children do not have the opportunity to spend money as they please. Parents may wish to supervise their purchases or advise them about how to use money they receive or earn. Or there simply may not be any "extra" for personal treats.

Grandma and grandpa can help out in this area. You don't have to be wealthy to do it. Nor does it mean crossing family boundaries. As you share, you can use that event as an opportunity to discuss money with your grandchildren—maybe even introduce them to some principles of wise earning, spend-ing, saving, comparison shopping, etc. You needn't be heavy-handed about it. But be ready to respond in a wise way if you get the chance.

Consider giving your grandchildren a couple of dollars to spend as they wish when they go shopping with you. Or tuck a dollar in an envelope with a note and tell them to buy a little treat "on" you. And of course, it would be important to allow for trial and error. That's how they'll learn. The more conservative grandchild might put the money into her bank for a future purchase. The spontaneous one is likely to buy the first thing he sees and then regret it. However they choose to respond, allow them to learn from it without adding your judgments or opinions—unless they ask for them.

You can help out financially in other ways too. My grandfather, for example, paid my weekly bowl-ing fee when I joined the high school team. He was a bowler during his retirement years, so it was quite special for him when I announced one night at the dinner table that I was taking up bowling. Right then he said he'd like to finance it. I'll never forget that. It forged a new connection between us. I was suddenly interested in his scores, and he was eager to hear mine.

Today, my children's father is paying the tuition for our grandson and granddaughter to take gymnastics lessons. He remembers with fondness the years our two daughters took gymnastics, and he wants to be a part of that tradition with our grandchildren. How nice for the children, and for their parents too. Money for such a luxury wouldn't have been readily available without Grandpa Jack's help.

While my children were young, I remember my parents inviting us to join them for part of their vacation. What a blessing for us. My husband was in law school during those early years, then setting up his practice. There wasn't much money for fancy vacations. Thanks to my parents, some of our fondest memories as a family were created during those times together.

Share your energy.
What are you saving it for?

One grandfather I spoke with spent so much energy trying to conserve his energy that I was amazed he was still alive. He did not like having active young children at his house. He didn't like surprises, and he preferred to sit rather than stand, observe rather than participate, hang back rather than step out.

Certainly there is room in the Grandparents' Club for people of every personality type and style—even couch potatoes—but those who are dedicated conservatives generally miss out on the love, the fun, the devotion, and the joy of making memories and building traditions with their grandchildren. If you are tempted to "take it easy," consider the fact that you will never pass this way again—and neither will your grandchildren.

Share your creativity. And watch it pop up in your grandchildren!

Granny Elizabeth is an amateur photographer. She's been snapping pictures for several decades and even has won an award for one of her photographs. She gave her grandson Graham a camera for his 10th birthday. Now the two of them go out shooting photos of every kind from portraits to parades.

Lauren's grandmother did some acting in community theater during her 20s and 30s. Now several decades later, 14-year-old Lauren is enrolled in a young adult theater in her town. Her grandmother is her biggest supporter.

"I've learned a lot from my grandma," said Lauren. "She's the only one in my family who knows what it feels like to be on stage, to become a character and bring that person to life. It's awesome. Grandma and I can talk for hours about the theater and whenever I want to see a play, she's game for it."

Lauren said her interest in acting started when she was a little girl of four or five. "Grandma used to help my brother and sister and me make up skits or playact a story from a book," Lauren said. "We had so much fun. I give her all the credit for introducing me to the theater."

Share your knowledge. Watch it take root.

Fifteen-year-old Roger is a Civil War buff largely because of his grandfather's passion for that period in history. Even as a little guy, he listened to his grandfather tell stories about the rivalry between the Confederates and the Yankees and how his home state of Kentucky tried to remain neutral and ended up hated by both sides.

Roger and his granddad subscribe to The History Book Club, sharing every book they can on the Civil War. They've traveled to some of the famous battle sites together, and Roger has enjoyed the benefit of his grandfather's expertise while he was researching a topic for a history project on the War.

"My grandfather and I are like this," said Roger, solidly holding his index and middle finger together.

What a privilege it is for Roger to have access to such knowledge. But it doesn't stop there. Some of the things his grandfather knows originated with an ancestor who served in the Confederacy during the Civil War. Roger not only has a partner to share his interest, but he's learning something about his family tree as well. You can't put a price on that kind of a gift. Consider what a memory and tradition that will be for Roger and for Roger's children when they come along someday.

Share your history. Give your grandchildren a sense of their roots.

About 10 years ago, I put together a framed collage of photos from each of my children's childhood. Today, they hang on the wall in their homes—a reference point for their children. At the time I assembled the photos, I wasn't a grandmother. But in my mind, I knew that somewhere down the line, this would be a gift to my grandchildren when they came along. The older ones, five and seven years old now, are beginning to recognize the various branches on the family tree through photos.

"This is Mom when she was five," says Johannah. "Pretty soon I'm gonna be five."

"Hey, Magah, you were my mother's mom." (Of course, I still am, as they are discovering.)

"Great-grammy is *your* mom, Magah?" What a discovery!

When they look at pictures of my mother, they have to stretch their minds a bit. To think that their grandmother with gray hair has a mother with white hair is quite a concept!

And they have another side of the family to investigate as well. On their dad's family tree there is a new host of people to sort out and get to know. But as they do so they are learning about themselves, where they came from, and what parts of themselves take root in those who have gone before them. Johannah has red hair like Uncle Kevin. Shevawn has the same name as her aunt who lives in Italy. Jacob has the same stocky build as the men in his dad's family.

All of these details are so interesting to children as they make connections during visits and reunions, celebrations and funerals. Grandparents can make an enormous contribution in this area. You are the keeper of the historical keys. Open the trunk of information and photos you have and invite your children's children to rummage through it with you.

I remember many happy hours spent at my in-laws' home going through albums and letters and documents from the past. My husband's children were fascinated with what Grandmom and Granddad Flowers had to share. And it was all the more relevant after his son and daughter actually went to Switzerland with their grandparents and visited the village where their great-grandfather had been raised.

But you don't have to board a plane or a boat to bring the past to life for your grandchildren. Oral stories, photos, journals, and letters can be good starting places.

You could assemble some of these items in an album or place them in a display box or cabinet as we have done (we call it the "family museum"). You can hang old photos on the wall, amid current pictures of your children and grandchildren.

We chose a wooden cabinet with glass doors to house some of our family "antiques," such as an old family Bible, bronzed baby shoes, my husband's first rattle, and his Shirley Temple breakfast bowl and cup. I have included my first walking shoes, my first dictionary given to me by my grandfather, and my first pair of earrings.

The grandmother of one young friend sent her a picture of a distant aunt. It was exciting for Luann to see how strong the resemblance was between herself and the woman named Ernestine. She was proud to display the picture and to point out to visitors and friends her connection with this great-aunt, even though they had never known each other in person.

You might also consider writing a chronology of events that highlighted your life as a child and include some appropriate photos to augment the autobiography. You could present it to the entire family (your children and their children) as a legacy to enjoy now and savor and reflect on after you're gone.

Consider some of these items to include:

- details about the United States and the world you grew up in

- a typical day at school
- "hot" fashions
- popular music with teens
- hobbies you pursued
- challenges you faced at different ages
- some facts about your relationship with your parents and siblings
- how you spent your leisure time
- friends you enjoyed
- a description of the house you grew up in
- best friends, boyfriends, and girlfriends
- details about your first date
- how you met your spouse
- some interesting jobs you've held
- the hopes and dreams you had for your future
- your relationship with God

Not only will your grandchildren (and your children too) get to know you better, but they will have a better sense of themselves as human beings. They will begin to see that life is a continuum, spanning the generations, and they are a vital part of it.

I remember how fascinated I was by my grandfather's account of his life as a boy in Ireland. He painted such a clear "word picture" of the house he grew up in that, when my parents visited the home years later, my mother was struck by how well-matched were my grandfather's descriptions and the reality of the place—even though more than 40 years had passed since he had been there.

Share your memories of them. What a gift!

Many parents today keep track of their children's lives through a journal, a running letter to each child to be given to them when they leave home, a baby book, photo albums, etc.

As a grandparent, you, too, may wish to document your viewpoint of each grandchild. What are your special memories of each one during the various stages of their lives? How would you like to bring those memories to life for yourself and for your grandchildren? Here are some ideas others have used successfully.

- *Memories on tape.* You can record your thoughts and feelings and reflections on audiocassette or videocassette. Make recordings at the births of your grandchildren, after a visit together, or following an event you attended with them such as a music recital, athletic event, family holiday, etc., or at any time you feel like expressing yourself to your grandchildren. You could present these as gifts each year or compile several and give them on a special occasion. Imagine how your grandchildren would feel to receive such a personal present.

- *Memories on paper.* One grandfather keeps a written record of his precious moments with his only granddaughter. Each event or experience they share is kept in the form of a letter. He tells Ellen his thoughts, feelings, observations, and remembrances about her. Sometimes he gives her a letter as a gift for a birthday or holiday. "But I always keep a copy in a box here at home," he said. "That way, when I'm gone, she'll have a whole set."

Max said his grandmother did something like that for him as a boy, and he has most of them to this day.

I have written a personal note or card to each of my grandchildren at their birth and their mothers have included them in the children's baby books.

- *Memories in a scrapbook.* You could do this project together with your grandchildren. When they reach school age, help them assemble important papers, documents, photos, ribbons, awards, etc., in a scrapbook. Add captions and comments and be sure to date the entries.

I never had a living grandmother as a child, but one of my aunts did something similar for me.

She compiled a photo album of snapshots of me throughout my life and captioned each page with a line from the famous poem "She Walks in Beauty." This was her wedding gift to me in 1960. I still have the album and it's a visual history of my life, as well as a scrapbook of memories that has blessed me and my children and now my grandchildren.

- *Memories on a wall.* Ethel P. has lined the stairway walls of her Ohio home with photo collages of children and grandchildren. At a glance, one can see the people, places, and events that make up the fabric of her family. She is a widow now, so the "memory wall," as she dubbed it, brings her special comfort and joy. There are pictures that span several decades, providing her children and grandchildren with a visual history of their heritage, from great-great-grandparents and aunts and uncles and cousins to contemporary relatives who live in various parts of the world.

Whatever way you choose to make memories and build traditions, the important thing is that you *do* something. If all these ideas seem overwhelming, pick out just one to start. Look at some of the things that were meaningful to you as a child. Think back to your own grandparents. What was special about them in your life? What memories and traditions did they leave with you? You may wish to activate those with your grandchildren.

If you did not have grandparents or they were passive in their relationship with you, then you have all the more reason to change that pattern in your relationship with your grandchildren. Time is short. They grow up quickly. Take action now to make memories and build traditions with your grandchildren that will enrich and deepen their lives and bless yours as well. And remember, there is no *one* way to do any of this. The idea is to select what's comfortable and appropriate for you. Our purpose is to grandparent—without guilt!

Making Connections

1. Choose one practical tool you received from this chapter and write a simple plan for implementing it in your relationship with your grandchildren. (For example: Keeping a journal, for each grandchild, of my impressions and feelings as he or she is growing up. I need to purchase three small blank books or loose-leaf notebooks. I'll start my entries next week after our family Thanksgiving.)

2. Think of one tradition that your parents or grandparents introduced you to as a child. How might you resurrect that with your grandchil-

dren so they will sense the links between generations? (For example: Each Christmas, my mother and I made and decorated gingerbread men from a recipe handed down to her from her grandmother. I still have that old recipe. I'd like to start that again with my grandchildren. *Or* I remember my grandfather's victory garden following World War II. Sometimes I helped him pick the vegetables or rake the ground. I'd like to teach my grandchildren how to create a little garden in their yard.)

3. Consider something that is important to you in your life today. How could you pass that on to your grandchildren? (For example: If you're a music or theater enthusiast, introduce your grandchildren to these experiences by taking them to a concert or ballet or stage play a couple of times a year. If you like to hike or fish or surf, take them along when they reach the appropriate age and teach them your skill.)

JUST THE TWO OF US

As I pulled into the restaurant parking lot in San Clemente, I could see red-headed Johannah peering out the window of the family van. Her mother and I had agreed to meet at this halfway point between our two Southern California homes. My four-year-old granddaughter would spend a couple of days with me—alone—and then I would drive her back to the same spot where her mother would pick her up.

We loaded her little duffel bag into my station wagon and swapped hugs and kisses with her mom and brothers. Then we were off—over the freeway and through the traffic to Grandmother's condo we drove!

As we approached San Diego about an hour later, I asked her what she'd like to do first. There was no hesitation. "The dollar store," she shouted. "I wanna go to the dollar store. Like we did last time."

"Then the dollar store it is," I said and drove down to the next exit. Within minutes we were inside—surrounded by toys and games and packaged groceries, party supplies, cards, household goods, and more. The best part was that everything was a dollar. In fact that's the name of the store, Everything's a Dollar. It's made for grandparents who want to "spoil" their grandchildren but not break their budget.

I handed Johannah two single dollar bills, one for each pocket of her purple corduroy jumper. "You choose how to spend it," I said. "Everything's a dollar."

"Wow!" she said. "That means I get two presents."

She fingered the money expectantly and then trotted down the aisle to the doll section. She made her selection quickly but then suddenly decided she had better check out the entire store before spending her precious dollars. What if she liked something better down that aisle or the next one or the next one?

So we made the rounds. But nothing could measure up to the beautiful doll with the long blond hair that she had spotted when we first walked in. Then she settled on a baby doll to go with the grown-up one. With dolls in hand, she walked up to the clerk, paid for her purchases, and off we went.

Our next stop? Crown Point Shores Park. But as we drove toward the parking lot, it began to rain. Scrap that plan. We had to think of another.

"Let's go to your house now," she said. "We can play dolls. I brought my other dolls too."

Within minutes, the two of us were seated comfortably on the floor of my bedroom playing dolls. The experience took me back nearly 50 years to the many rainy afternoons when my sister and I and the two neighbor girls played dolls by the hour.

Suddenly Johannah broke into my reverie. "Magah," she said, "isn't it fun being by ourselves without Noah and Jacob (her brothers) bugging us?"

I agreed. It was fun indeed.

We went to the video store and rented a movie. We had dinner in the den, a special treat, and a cozy bath in our open tub (the kids call it Magah's swimming pool). And there was lots of time for snuggling and reading before bed. We even made a blueberry pie (even though I'm a grandmother who gave up baking)! It didn't turn out very well, but we had fun doing it—just the two of us—together.

As I recount this experience, I am struck by how simple yet special our visit was. Johannah went home thoroughly happy, and I felt completely refreshed. But most important, we had connected where it counts. We had spent quality time alone—just the two of us.

I had made the time and I had the desire to indulge her long shopping spree, the dolls spread out in my bedroom, and the blueberry juice on the kitchen floor. We had no deadlines to meet, no reason to hurry, and no boundaries we couldn't bend, if we wanted to.

On another weekend a year or so before, Johannah's older brother, Noah, had come down to my home for an overnight visit. Before we even parked the car in my driveway, he said, "Magah, isn't this fun—just the two of us?" We hadn't even gone to the museum's whale exhibit yet or to the park or to the beach. The important thing to him was that whatever we did it would be special because it was just the two of us.

A Couple of Pals

I can't say enough good things about the value of spending time alone with one grandchild at a time. Not both grandparents and one child, though there is a place for that too. But one-on-one—or as my grandchildren say, "just the two of us."

People of all ages are hungry for undivided personal time with one of their loved ones. Wives want more time alone with their husbands. Husbands want time alone with their wives. Kids want to feel special to individual parents, and parents want to connect with their children in a personal way. But somehow life—the daily routine—what I call the "have tos," get in the way.

There's work and laundry and food shopping and school and Little League and piano lessons and PTA meetings and church and Sunday school ... and well, you know how it goes. Weeks and months slip by to the point that some families feel waving hi and bye is the extent of their contact.

But grandparents have the unique opportunity to come into their grandchildren's home and take them out—one at a time—for a quality "just-the-two-of-us" visit. It doesn't require money or even much time. It does require, however, that you *be* there, present to the child as a person who cares, who listens, who empathizes, who affirms, who is fun, and who is easy to be with.

That can take place over a pancake breakfast at a local diner or on the floor of your bedroom playing dolls. It can happen while you drive to the grocery or hardware store or in a shared moment during a symphony or play.

Whatever you choose, make sure it's something for just the two of you. By the way, sitting on a bench reading a newspaper while your grandchild plays alone in the sand at the park is not what I'm talking about! Dropping your grandchild off at a library event for children and then picking him up later doesn't count either.

Just-the-two-of-us means just that—you and your grandchild together, interacting, doing something, perhaps, or just hanging out, walking and talking.

Grandparent Calendar

Fine for you to say, you may be thinking, but I'm a career person and I hardly have enough time to see my children and grandchildren as a group, let alone one on one.

I understand. My life is full and busy too. But if you want to have more than a polite and distant relationship with your grandchildren, I believe it's essential to find ways to interact with them one at a time.

Here are some possibilities to consider.

- While attending a family group event, sneak away after the meal with one of the kids and go for a walk—alone. *Or* take the toddler to a nearby park for a few minutes on the swing and slide.

- Offer to take one child out for a meal or to the library or a museum for a couple hours. Then bring him home. You might be amazed at how special a time you'll both have even in a short span of time.

- Sign up for a class with one of your older grandchildren. This is a great way to spend time together. Poppy Lou loves to play chess, according to his grandson Blake. Lou taught Blake the basics of the game. Then the two of them took a chess class together at a local club.

- Combine business and pleasure. For example, in January I'll be teaching a weekend workshop in a town near my oldest daughter's home. An idea that occurs to me is to invite one of my grandchildren to join me. On my way to the hotel, I could swing by her house and pick up my grandson or granddaughter. Then we can have dinner together, swim in the indoor pool, and spend the night together. Mom and Dad and the others can join us for breakfast and then take the child home before I go off to work. It will require some planning and some extra effort—but it's worth it. Not often do I have such an opportunity. Some variation of this might work for you.

A grandmother I know signed up for a convention in Big Bear, California, during February one year. She thought it would be great fun to have her 10-year-old granddaughter come along because the girl lived in Arizona and seldom saw the snow. But what would she do all day while grandma was in the seminar sessions? My friend invited her retired husband along. He agreed to spend time with Amanda during the day when she could have fun in the snow. The three of them would have dinner together at night. Then Grandpa could enjoy the quiet of the room in the evening while Grandma and Amanda visited, one-on-one, in the fireside room, playing cards and board games.

Takes a bit of planning? Sure! Was it worth it? Ask Amanda. "I got to spend time alone with both my grandma and my grandpa," she said. "It was great!"

Stephen and Janet Bly, authors of *How to Be a*

Good Grandparent (Moody, 1990), suggest that grandparents plan their calendar a year in advance. With a "Grandparent Calendar" in place, you are more likely to carry out the plans that you may now simply hold in your mind or heart. Visits with our grandchildren don't just happen. Like everything else in life, we have to get them underway with a bit of strategic and advance planning.

I try to see my four grandchildren who live within a hundred miles of me at least once a month. Sometimes all I can manage is a two- or three-hour stopover on my way to a teaching appointment. Even then, I try to have a little time with each one individually.

Johannah and I can almost always squeeze in a game of Shadow Tag. Baby Liam is content with a few minutes of uninterrupted holding. Noah and I can color or cut and paste or build something together. And Jacob is happy if I read him a story that he picks out.

And Shevawn, my granddaughter who lives several hundred miles away, is just as important to me as the others, even though I don't see her as often. But even with this greater distance between us, I've managed to spend time with her every two or three months since she was born 15 months ago.

The Grandparent Calendar has really worked for me. (Thanks Stephen and Janet!) I teach weekend writing courses three times a year in the Northern

California town where Shevawn and her parents, my daughter Erin and her husband, Bruce, live. Naturally, I stay with them instead of a hotel during those weekends.

My husband and I also pay attention to the fluctuating airfares. We recently flew to their town for half price. That price made it less expensive to fly than to drive and took a lot less time. And Erin and Shevawn have come to San Diego twice as well. We share the airfare, making it a good deal for everyone. But none of this would happen if we didn't plan ahead and keep ourselves aware of the possibilities.

I used to envy retired grandparents who had the freedom to do as they pleased. I assumed that part of their pleasure would be to visit their grandchildren as often as possible. But one retired grandfather told me that he actually sees the children less than when he was working. Why? Because he and his wife have joined the RV set, and they travel out of state several times a year for extended periods.

It was then that I realized that sometimes those of us who have the fullest schedules accomplish more of what we want because we have to plan in order to meet our goals.

Ideas for Just the Two of You

- *Infants and babies.* Hold, rock, read to, sing to, or take them for a walk in a stroller or baby carrier.

These activities have been my favorites with Shevawn and our newest grandchildren, Liam and Rachel.

- *Toddlers and preschoolers.* Play with blocks, building equipment, and toys. Read books, swim, run, take them to the park, do simple cooking or baking together.

- *Primary-grade children.* Invite them to stay overnight. Include some simple but special activities you can do together: bake cookies or muffins; go swimming; visit the library, museums, or public parks. Give them a dollar or two to spend as they wish at a variety store. Make a picnic lunch together and eat it at the park.

- *Youth and preteens.* Boys and girls ages 8 to 12 enjoy some of the same things named for primary-grade children, but you can expand the experiences to meet their age and interest levels. For example, these children might like to enroll in a program at a park whereas a younger child may be content with just a short play time at the park.

Older children also enjoy cooking projects and unlike the younger ones, could actually help you fix an entire meal. They also like to have gift money to spend as they wish. From time to time, ask what they would do with $5 or $10 or $50. You will find out their interests and preferences this way and get some ideas for Christmas and birthday gifts.

In fact, shopping together for a large, wanted gift item is a great way to spend time with an older grandchild. For example, if you offer to buy a bicycle or musical instrument or to pay for a summer camp, you could spend your time together researching the purchase or project.

If you invite older grandchildren on a trip—especially to another state or country as my in-laws did with my husband's children—make them partners in the planning stage. Look at maps and travel guides together and plan the itinerary to include activities that everyone will enjoy.

One of my friends took her youngest son to Europe when he was 12. She let him take his in-line skates along. She liked to bicycle so the two of them had a great time rolling along the paths and roads of France and Holland. A grandparent could consider a similar trip. If you're no longer up to in-line skating or bike riding, how about a walking or hiking tour?

One 85-year-old grandfather and great-grandfather led members of three generations of his family up Mt. Whitney (the highest peak in the lower 48 states) last summer.

Age shouldn't be an excuse for not being active on a one-on-one basis with our grandchildren. Even someone who is housebound or bedridden can enjoy the relationship. All it really takes is two people spending time together. This can include an activity, but it doesn't have to.

- *Teenagers and young adults.* Grandchildren in these age groups frequently have busy lives of their own. It may be more difficult to reach them for private visits. But you can still make the effort. I believe they will appreciate your desire to stay connected. By the time they reach high school, if you are still able, they may enjoy a dinner or theater date with you, a short trip where they can participate in the choice, or your presence at one of their games or other high school events. You can help them research a college or university to attend, offering your advice and experience. Then visit them at college and stay close through letters and phone calls.

The consistent presence of a grandparent in a child's life, from birth to adulthood and beyond, is a blessing that cannot be measured. I have a 42-year-old friend whose grandmother is now 104. According to my friend Abby, her grandmother is just now beginning to lose interest in life. She's refusing to eat and talking about dying. Abby is feeling the loss deeply. This is not just an old woman who is dying after a long and full life. This woman is Abby's dear grandmother for whom she will truly mourn.

More Ideas for Just the Two of You

Following is a collection of ideas that grandparents have shared. You can choose those that interest you and match them appropriately with your grandchildren.

- *Start a hobby together.* Collect stamps or teacups, bottle caps or greeting cards. Join a bird-watching club. Paint or sketch together. Learn about whales and go on a whale-watching excursion.

- *Volunteer for public service.* Feed the homeless. Pick up trash in a local park. Help with a political campaign. Plant greenery along the highway. Pick up goods from neighbors for recycling.

- *Invite your grandchild to spend a day at work with you.* Give him or her a behind-the-scenes tour of your facility and what your work involves. Go out for lunch and answer any questions he or she may have.

- *Put together a family recipe book to share with parents, aunts, uncles, and cousins.* Ask each family member to contribute favorite recipes. Include a picture of each contributor.

- *Participate in a church choir, skit, vacation Bible school, or family camp together.* Even though you will be among other people, the experience of just the two of you, as opposed to you and all the grandkids in the family, will be special.

- *Plant a flower or vegetable garden together.* If neither of you have a yard, you can do a window garden. Perhaps you could start one at each of your homes, and then help each other keep the garden going and growing.

- *Plan a surprise for a member of the family.* One year, my aunt took one of my children aside and the two of them cooked up a little party to celebrate our dog's first birthday. Erin was a preschooler at the time, so this was a very special event to her. Now, as I reflect on that wonderful surprise, complete with horns and party hats and lemonade and cake, I see this as an idea that any grandparent could apply.

- You could extend this to a surprise meal for mom and dad after a day away from home, a surprise party for someone's birthday, a surprise poster with pictures for Mothers' Day or Fathers' Day, and so on.

Making Connections

1. Consider the ideas mentioned in this chapter. Which ones can you use now and which ones would you use in the future to build a series of visits over your grandkids' lifetimes that are just for the two of you?

2. Make a Grandparent Calendar. Depending on how many grandchildren you have and their ages, plan specific ways for you to spend time with each one alone during the course of the year. Consult parents so you can coordinate your schedules. You may have to make some adjustments along the way, but with ideas in writing, you're likely to accomplish most, if not all, of the plans you make.

3. Ask each of your grandchildren to tell you or give you a list of ways they'd like to spend time with you. You might be surprised and delighted by the suggestions they make. Act on the ones that are appropriate. And remember, whatever you do, do it with a sense of joy, never guilt. Who we are with our grandchildren is always more important than what we do.

7

GRANDPARENTING ACROSS THE MILES

I had the privilege of seeing my one grandfather nearly every day of my childhood. He moved in with our family when I was a toddler and died years after I was married and had moved away.

My children, on the other hand, lived their entire childhoods miles away from both sets of grandparents. Yet my son and two daughters to this day say they felt very close to their grandparents—especially to my parents—who went well beyond what most people would do to build and maintain their relationship with my children.

They wrote to their grandchildren regularly, they visited them at least once a year either at our home or theirs, they phoned frequently, and they sent unexpected treats and wonderful gifts for special occasions. Often they invited our family to join them at a dude ranch, a resort, or a hotel for a few days of fun together somewhere between our two hometowns.

My husband's parents were less expressive in terms of travel, but their love was sincere and their many ways of displaying it were touching. They, too, enjoyed participating on a variety of levels. They bought the kids bedroom furniture, a sewing machine for me so I could make the girls' clothes, and they welcomed us to their home whenever we could go to Illinois for a visit. Meals were generous and beds were cozy and comfortable.

I have wonderful memories of both sets of parents embracing the children and giving them a sense of heritage in the ways that best expressed their identity and ability.

I did miss having my mother and father close by to share the day-to-day experiences, such as shopping for school clothes with the children, decorating for Christmas, attending a school play or a church event together. But they were still grandparents—and great ones—in every sense of the word. Both my parents and my in-laws were good models for me to look at when my first two grandchildren lived on the other side of the world and now, when my youngest grandchild lives at the other end of the state.

It takes more effort to grandparent across the miles than it does to be next door or down the street or within an hour's drive. But we can all do it, if we want to. And from the experience of my own children, I know how worthwhile it is. My children will truly mourn the loss of my parents when they die, as they did when their father's parents passed away years ago.

And what about the benefits for us, the grandparents? Only each one of us knows the answer to that question. My hunch is that it is just as important for us to be friends with our grandchildren as it is for them to become friends with us. But to bring this about, you must make it happen. Here are some ideas that other "long-distance" grandparents have shared.

Calling All Grandchildren

The telephone is an obvious first thought. You can talk to your grandchildren nearly everywhere in the world thanks to the legacy of Alexander Graham Bell. Then again, maybe you can't. Or it's not easy. When my daughter and her husband lived in Morocco, they didn't have a telephone. To reach them, I had to call their landlady and hope she would agree to let them use her phone. That required some planning in terms of time, her work schedule, family meals, etc. And when I did call, I hoped that her availability fit with my daughter's.

As a result, we didn't speak often—perhaps once a month or less. Occasionally, Julie would call me from a public phone, but even then our conversations were short and somewhat strained. At the time, my grandson Noah was under two years of age so I could say no more than a few words to him anyway, but not having access to them by telephone as often as I wanted was very difficult.

If you face this situation yourself, then you may want to rely on other methods mentioned in this chapter. But if you can call your grandchildren and their parents as frequently as you wish, do so. It's a privilege we probably take for granted until we don't have it.

Following are some suggestions for making the most of your telephone visits.

Plan your calls.

Find out your grandchildren's routines: school hours, meals, bedtimes, weekend activities, church, etc. Some grandparents pick up the phone at their convenience only and then wonder why they sometimes get a poor reception or the call is cut short.

Avoid small talk.

"How's the weather? We're having a downpour here."

"What have you been up to?"

"Sure is hard to nail you down. Seems you're gone most of the time."

Awkward passages like these would never even occur to a grandparent who:

- knows what the grandchildren are doing at school and in their leisure time

- remembers the names of some of their best friends

- shares a hobby or interest with the grandchildren such as music or sewing or skiing or stamp collecting
- understands where the grandchildren are spiritually
- recalls important events and dates in their lives

If you have access to all this information, you'll have food for many interesting phone conversations. To remain current, keep a notepad handy as you're speaking. Write down the names of their new friends and the date of the basketball tournament or the school play. Then you'll not only be prepared to call and ask how the event turned out, but you might even send a fax or a bouquet of flowers to celebrate the occasion.

Talk about yourself.

It's important to foster a two-way relationship. Let your grandchildren know the names of some of your friends and the important dates in your life. Ask the older ones for their advice or their perspective on something. "What kind of sandwiches would a teenage youth group like? I'm in charge of refreshments" or "If you wanted a couple of days off work and you'd used up all your vacation time, how would you ask your boss? I could use a little help with this."

Look forward to something together.

If you see your grandchildren during the holidays or you're planning a trip to their house next summer, mention this on the phone. Let them participate in the planning. Depending on their age, you can ask them to get information about a play you want to see with them or a tour of a historic building or a side trip to the ocean or whatever. Notice how you and your grandchildren will draw closer as you plan your visit and anticipate it together.

Rediscover Letter Writing

In this age of advancing technology, the art of letter writing may seem a bit old-fashioned—to everyone except the recipient, that is. Many of those who do not like to *write* letters are the same people who like to *receive* them.

I doubt there's a person alive who doesn't enjoy finding a letter addressed to him or her in the daily mail. Grandparents and grandchildren are no different.

Young Robin flips through the morning mail and spots Gram's handwriting on the envelope addressed to her. "Mom, Mom, I got a letter from Gram," she shouts, waving the envelope over her head.

A couple of weeks later, it's Gram who gets excited when she sees Robin's familiar handwriting on an envelope addressed to her. "Well, look at this," she says to her husband. "A letter from Robin. I wonder what she has to say. She's enclosed her school picture too."

If you'd like to revive the art of letter writing in your family, here are some suggestions to apply.

- *Match your letter to the child's age and experience.* A short one-page note in large bold print will delight a toddler or preschooler. If he can't read it himself, he'll know it's for him when mother or dad reads it to him. Add a stick of gum or a page of stickers and he'll be thoroughly delighted. Or how about a few computer graphics like Granny L's teddy bears?

- *Lengthen your letters appropriately for older children.* Again, avoid small talk. If you know some facts about their lives and their friends and their activities, mention them. Ask questions. Tell them you'll be pulling for their team to win, and you'll be praying for a good result in their spelling test.

- *Add a few details about your life and ask for their prayers too.* Be sure to end every letter by expressing your love. No one on the face of the earth can hear the words "I love you" too often. It's one way we can afford to thoroughly spoil one another—especially our grandchildren.

- *Create quick notes by keeping a stack of pre-stamped postcards (buy them at the post office) in a handy place.* This written correspondence is less personal than a letter, but it can be a good link between letters. And it can take the place of a letter when you are in a hurry.

- *Speed your correspondence over the miles with a fax, if you and your grandchildren have access to one.* You also can help a grandchild with homework, create a report, or generate a necessary response to some inquiry by using the fax to communicate. I don't believe this option takes the place of the mailed letter, but it's a fine option to have.

- *Increase your chances of getting a reply by sending your grandchildren stationery or note cards as an occasional gift.* Add a good ballpoint pen and a book of stamps and they'll have no excuse not to write you! One desperate and humorous grandmother sent her college-bound granddaughter a stack of stamped scenic postcards and a stamp (for a stamp pad) that read *Having a great time. Wish you were here. Love, Sheila.*

"It worked," said her grandmother. "I think she got the message that I wanted to hear from her because I presented it in a playful way. She did send me the cards, and occasionally, she even added a note of her own. I was satisfied."

Get It on Tape (or film or both)

Photos, audiocassettes, videocassettes—whatever the state of the art, get acquainted with it. I guarantee you your grandkids will know about it. Noah knew how to handle the VCR before he was two years old. In fact, he taught me how to insert, eject, rewind, and fast forward before he could even read the labels.

There's nothing more wonderful than to see and hear your grandchildren who live across the miles. Every time we got a new videocassette and saw how the children had grown, I cried. The months were zipping by, and the kids were zipping up in size and stature, in vocabulary, and in physical ability. I missed being there for all these milestones. But the next best thing was certainly the wonderful videocassettes my son-in-law sent every few months.

Your grandchildren may have the same longing to talk to and touch you as you do for them. Return the favor. Shoot a few sessions with your video camera or borrow or rent one. Speak directly to the kids just as you would if they were there in person. Pull up a chair and a storybook and read them a story. My daughter said my grandson listened to and watched my tapes over and over.

I also sent one audiocassette of me reading a favorite book. I sent the book along for him to follow as he listened to me reading. But I forgot to do one thing I recommend to you. If your grandchild is not yet able to read, ring a little bell or blow a whistle each time you turn the page. That will be the child's signal to do the same.

"Care" Packages

Everyone loves a gift. Sometimes the more spontaneous and unexpected, the better. Kids, especially, love surprises. As I was writing this chapter, I got up and went to the store to buy some cards. It's nearly Halloween, and I want to send my grandchildren a card, a note, and a little "treat" since we don't live close enough for them to ring my doorbell.

The entire investment was less that $7. I bought a small card for each one, a package of sugarless chewing gum, and a sheet of Halloween stickers. This is just about right for children under 8 years old. Older kids would appreciate $5 or $10 and a note or card.

Between birthdays and holidays, surprise your grandchildren once in awhile with a "care" package that is unique to you. Maybe you like to work with wood or do needlework or you create crossword puzzles or other word games on paper. Perhaps you're known for your lemon poppyseed cake or, like my sister, you make marvelous honey-bran muffins. Make a batch and send them along (including the recipe so they can duplicate the gift and share it with others). Remember Grandma Bonnie's peanut butter cookies? Grandson Andrew sure does!

Grandchildren of any age would enjoy a book or a magazine or even a few pictures cut from a magazine that they could make into a colorful collage. *Or* you could make one for them and send it along with a note saying these pictures remind you of them.

If you are feeling stuck for ideas for what you could do, here's a few suggestions to consider for each month of the year. If you want to plan ahead, so they receive a gift from you on a regular basis, select what you want to do or buy and enter it on your Grandparent Calendar.

Buy greeting cards on sale or by the box and keep a good supply of postage stamps on hand. Last week I found a wonderful sale at the local Christian bookstore. Now I've got enough birthday cards to last the whole year and for a great price too.

Following is a sample Grandparent Calendar of simple, inexpensive ways to let your grandchildren know you're thinking of them. Feel free to add additional ideas under each month.

January

- A new pair of mittens or a snow hat (for cold climate)
- A book to curl up with
- A bag of colored popping corn and hot cider mix
- $5 or $10 in spending money

February

- A new CD (check with parents to avoid duplication)
- Money for a movie with a friend
- A roll of film and money for processing
- A box of homemade cookies or a cake

March

- A tablet and monogrammed pencils or a coloring book and crayons
- A love note stuck in a new pair of socks
- A picture of you and your spouse in a little frame
- A packet of flower seeds for a window garden

April

- Some personal items: toothbrush, hand lotion, cologne, lipstick
- A tulip plant in bloom delivered by a florist
- A gift certificate for lunch at a favorite restaurant
- A videocassette of you and your spouse

May

- A small album with some recent photos
- A favorite recipe from your file

- A homemade bookmark with the child's name or initials
- A craft kit from a hobby store

June

- Colored pencils and a sketch pad
- A water gun
- A pack of sugarless bubble gum
- A new swimsuit or beach towel

July

- A sticker set and a sticker book to put them in
- A package of lemonade mix
- A small toy (doll, jump rope, Frisbee, beach ball, sand pail)
- Tickets to a water slide, miniature golf, or amusement park (call the facility and order by phone)

August

- A T-shirt, new pair of shorts, a sun hat or sunglasses
- A paperback book by a favorite author
- A picture frame
- A little box for storing treasures

September

- School supplies (find out what's needed and wanted)
- A new pen and pencil set
- An inexpensive wristwatch
- A pocket-size dictionary

October

- A selection of colorful autumn leaves (if available)
- A poem or story you wrote
- A box of notecards and postage stamps
- A blank book for keeping a diary

November

- A disposable camera and money for processing
- A new belt, scarf, necklace, or earrings
- Bubble bath or cosmetics
- Money to put towards camp or youth retreat

December

- A calendar for the new year
- A toddler, youth, or student Bible
- A personalized ornament for the Christmas tree
- A book of meditations for the new year

There's no substitute for being there in person, for cuddling your grandkids on your lap, for chasing toddlers around the living room furniture, for holding the newborn in your arms, for planting the flower seeds together, for praying for each other on the spot, or for shopping for a new bike or book with one another. But since the miles separate you, do the next best thing—skip over the miles with a phone call, an audiocassette or videocassette, a letter, or a gift.

Grandparenting across the miles takes a little more effort and ingenuity than being there in person, but it can be done successfully and easily with a little planning. And you and your grandchildren will be the richer and the closer for it.

Making Connections

1. Include on your Grandparent Calendar when you will call, send audiocassettes or videocassettes, cards, letters, or gifts to your grandchildren. Make it a point to connect with each one in one way or another at least once a month.

2. Watch for sale items, especially toys, books, and cards, at your local stores. With an eye on what's ahead on your calendar, buy in advance when appropriate so you'll have a ready supply when needed.

3. Buy two maps, one of the United States (or the country where you live) and one of your city or town. Mark the state and town where you live on the U.S. map and do the same for the town where your grandchildren live. Then mark the city map with colored dots to indicate the places where you work, go to church, play golf, swim, etc. Send the maps to your grandchildren. Ask them to get a map of their community and mark the places where they go to school, play soccer, take piano lessons, go on vacation, etc. This is another great way to link your household to theirs and to keep the connection across the miles.

PART 3

THE TOUGH ISSUES: LIVING WITH CHALLENGES

8

GRANDPARENTS RAISING GRANDCHILDREN

Lou and Martha raised their granddaughter from infancy through college. "From the time she was a baby," said Martha, "she bonded with us, not her mother.

"Our daughter started doing drugs again after Mandy was born. We'd go over to her apartment and nearly gag," Martha said. "Trash was overflowing. There was no fresh air. Cigarette butts and the smell of smoke filled the room. The baby always needed a diaper change."

"At first, we tried not to see it as bad as it was," Lou interrupted. "Gloria is our daughter, and we love her. She made mistakes—having a baby without being married, getting in with the wrong crowd, and doing drugs in high school. But we thought all that was behind her when she had the baby. We didn't want to make her feel worse. We hoped she'd get things together, and we believed she would if we helped out. We gave her money. We baby-sat. We took Mandy on weekends."

But it never got better, according to Martha and Lou. It got worse.

"We noticed cigarette burns on the baby's bottom, and she seemed dazed, unresponsive. She did not develop like other children," said Lou. "She was late in sitting up, crawling, and walking. And she seemed scared of quick movements. We noticed early on that we had to speak softly and slowly and be real gentle with her or she'd scream."

"Sometimes she screamed anyway," added Martha, as she wiped at the tears that clouded her eyes. "And she was afraid of men. Even Lou at first. We think our daughter's boyfriend may have hurt the baby, too, though we could never prove it."

All Too Common

Martha and Lou's story is not unusual—not to other parents raising grandchildren. Drugs are the reason, more than any other, that children are living with their grandparents. Eighty to 90 percent of the custody cases involve drug or alcohol abuse, according to Mignon Scherer, marriage and family therapist and founder and director of the San Diego support group Grandparents Raising Grandchildren.

Scherer shared literature citing Census Bureau statistics that show approximately 3.3 million children lived with grandparents in 1991—a 44 percent increase since 1980. One million grandparents are currently raising grandchildren by themselves, and another 1.5 million have taken in their grandchildren as well as their children. That accounts for five percent of American families.

Different but Not Inferior

But the statistics are mere numbers if you have not experienced it yourself. Scherer agrees. She knows firsthand what it's like to raise a grandchild. To have a daughter on drugs. To be torn between "the light of her life"—her little grandson—her daughter whom she loved, the disruption to her household, the worry and fear and anger and turmoil.

When the situation became intolerable, she and her husband opened their home to their four-year-old grandson. "What started out to be six months," Scherer said, "turned into 10 years."

The social worker said theirs was the toughest case she ever saw. After five hearings, the Scherers gained legal guardianship, and their grandson lived with them until this year. Currently, he is living on a working ranch and loving it. He is recovering from drug abuse and learning how to integrate with other people in a healthy environment.

Understandably, Scherer was reluctant to share too many details, but she did say that whatever the cost—financial, emotional, mental, or physical—it was worth it.

"I never felt as if we were sacrificing anything," Scherer said. "We didn't consider it a sacrifice. Our life was different but not inferior."

Wanted: Recognition and Legal Support

The experience with her grandson propelled Scherer into working with her weekly support group with other grandparents who are raising grandchildren. That group led to the foundation of another organization for grandparents called GOLD (Grandparents Offering Love and Direction). Founded and directed by Margie Davis, the group focuses on guiding grandparents through the legal system as they seek custody, financial support, and social services.

"Our lawmakers must be willing not only to give us the responsibility of caring for our families' children in time of crisis, but they also must be willing to give us the rights that must accompany such responsibility and support," said Davis to a roomful of grandparent guardians,

Sharon and Larry J. of Minnesota agree. They know from experience what it's like to need assistance and not be able to get it.

"We were told we could not receive any financial help until we drew out my husband's IRA and used it up," Sharon said. "That made me angry. We were not seeking assistance for ourselves. It would cost the government a lot less to have our two granddaughters in our home than in foster care, daycare, or under the care of the county or state."

When Sharon and Larry decided to take custody of their favorite M and Ms—Melissa and Michelle—they were in it for the long haul, through their college years. It wouldn't be easy. Neither Sharon nor Larry was retired. They did not have a large income. In fact, both grandparents were students themselves at the time. They needed financial help if they were to raise Melissa and Michelle.

Larry said they should have required child support from the parents from the very beginning. They were in contact with both their son and the children's mother. But they did not require it because, as Larry said, "We wanted it to come from their parents because they wanted to take care of their children, not because it was ordered."

But God provided despite the lack of responsibility on the parents' part. "I used our local food shelf, picked up surplus food whenever our county was handing it out, planted a garden, and accepted veggies and other groceries from family members and friends," said Sharon.

"Our church family passed down dresses for the girls," added Sharon. "And just when our needs were the greatest, we'd often find packages of frozen meat or vegetables or an envelope with cash waiting on the front seat of our car when we came out of church."

All in all, Larry and Sharon agree that raising grandchildren "is a labor of love, truly sacrificial." But Sharon advises grandparents to obtain legal custody of their grandchildren if they decide they are going to raise them.

"Children need the security of knowing where they belong," she said. "Legal custody also makes it easier to receive the help and support you will need through the years.

"If there is any group of people today who need an encouraging word, a pat on the back and understanding," Sharon added, "it's the grandma and grandpa who decided to put the interests of a child before their own."

Custody hearings, financial assistance, and legal rights, important as they are, however, are not the only things on a grandparent's mind. At Scherer's support group, men and women discuss the challenges, but they also talk freely about the joys they experience in raising the younger generation. Many agree the children keep them younger mentally, and they feel good inside knowing they are providing a stable and loving home for their grandchildren.

After speaking with several men and women who, like the Scherers and Sharon and Larry, have raised grandchildren, two things stuck in my mind:

- *Love* is the driving force for taking the children;
- Raising grandchildren is just plain hard work.

There is no getting around the reality of the everyday challenges. And there is no denying the deep well of love these grandparents have for their child's child.

One woman put it best when she said, "Child of my child is twice my child."

The Hardest Thing I Ever Did

Agnes H. knows about the love and about the hard work involved in raising grandchildren. Soft-spoken, with expressive brown eyes and a delightful British accent, Agnes shared the story of how her two granddaughters, Susan and Mae, came to live with her and her husband, Jack.

"Our youngest daughter was 18 when Susan was born," she said. "We had the baby with us off and on since her birth in 1983. Things were difficult from the very beginning."

Their daughter had been abusing drugs for several years, as was the child's father. Eventually, the two broke up, but it didn't change things for the better. "She just took up with another druggie," said Agnes.

Agnes and Jack helped their daughter by taking Susan to and from school each day. And after Mae was born in 1986 and William in 1987, Agnes had the children for weekends and outings. During these visits, they began noticing how uncommunicative their grandchildren were.

"The little one, Mae, a toddler at the time, stood facing the wall at our house. She wouldn't talk. She wouldn't move," Agnes said. "It was as though she were scared all the time, afraid she'd be hurt if she spoke up or entered into the activities."

Gradually, Mae's behavior changed as she began to feel safe around her grandparents, but for a long time, she appeared suspicious of everyone. More and more often, Agnes and Jack saw signs of physical abuse, especially on Mae. They noticed burns on different parts of her body, she was quick to cry and scream, and she resisted being held.

Agnes' daughter would not discuss the problem. "She told us we made her feel guilty so she couldn't talk about it. I knew I couldn't stand by and do nothing," Agnes said. "So I called Child Protective Services. It was one of the hardest things I ever did.

"We had to build a case file," she added. "So I called the agency constantly, whenever I saw another sign of abuse."

Each time Agnes and Jack took the children back to their mother after a visit, "they'd look at us as if we, too, had betrayed them. They knew that we knew what was going on," said Agnes.

What they didn't understand, however, was that

their grandparents couldn't simply keep them. They had to gain custody through the legal system. Unless they followed the rules, they risked losing the children completely.

"Our daughter can charm the birds out of the trees," said Agnes, raising her eyes to heaven. "She could put on quite an act for the social worker if she wanted to."

Then one night, Susan phoned in tears. "I can't stay here anymore," she said.

In that moment, Agnes and Jack knew they had to take action. "The poor little girl had been a mother to the others," said Agnes. "And she couldn't do it anymore."

The social worker assigned to their case did everything she could to speed up the custody process. The children moved in with Agnes and Jack when the girls were six and three and their little brother was about two years old.

"Actually, we had tried *not* to take them permanently," said Agnes. "I guess that sounds terrible, doesn't it? But we didn't think we could do it. My husband had retired. We had plans for our own life after raising our four kids. And we were older and had less energy than when we were raising our children."

Agnes and Jack knew that if the children were to survive, they had to take them in. "I couldn't have done it without my spiritual faith," Agnes said with a deep sigh. "So many things were out of my hands.

"You've heard the saying, 'Let go and let God?' It sounds like a cliché, but it works," Agnes said. "Whenever I prayed and turned the situation over to God, it seemed easier."

Agnes talked about the daily routine of life as a grandparent raising grandchildren. "At first, all three lived with us, but after a couple of weeks, we knew we couldn't manage them all," Agnes said. So the children's other grandfather—their dad's father—agreed to take William.

"Bless his heart," she added with a smile. "The man was 66 at the time, living alone, and suddenly, he had a two-year-old to raise. But we're so grateful to him. We felt supported."

Agnes' eyes teared as she shared the challenges. "The hardest part," she said, "was the emotional pain. Mae had been locked in a closet, burned with cigarettes, and thrown against walls. When she came with us, she screamed day and night for months. It was as though she finally felt safe enough to let out her terrifying feelings."

The younger ones, especially, needed lots of contact. "They climbed in bed with us every morning. I hugged them a lot, especially Mae," Agnes recalled. "She had to know I was sincere. When she turned to the wall or screamed, I just put my arms around her and held her. And we gave her a pillow and a stuffed animal to pound on."

Her grandchildren began calling Agnes "Mommy," but she didn't feel right about that. It was important that they know who their real mother was, even if it was grandmother who was doing the "mothering."

The children went to a psychiatrist twice a week for months. "I think it helped," she said, "though later Susan, the older girl, said she could talk to me even better.

"Watching them suffer, crying for their mother, listening to the lies their mother told them," Agnes' voice trailed off as she thought about that first year. "One thing I learned quickly is not to criticize the children's mother in front of them.

"When they asked why she didn't want them, I told them she was sick, that she couldn't take care of them right now," Agnes said. "Then I'd reassure them that we would take care of them and that we loved them. It's so important to tell them you love them. They need to know that."

The children saw their mother occasionally under supervision. And Agnes said she did call them once in awhile, but they never knew when to expect it. Today, she lives somewhere in Northern California with a gang, and she's still doing drugs.

"When things finally evened out," Agnes concluded, "it was just a lot of hard work!" But the children began to respond to the security of a routine and a regular schedule.

Agnes smiled as she talked about their remarkable progress over the past few years. Susan made the honor role at school this year. Mae is in the "gifted" program. And little William is doing well living with his grandfather and more recently with his natural father, who is now clean and sober and ready to take on his parental responsibilities. The girls moved in with him and their brother at the end of the last school term and, Agnes acknowledged, "They're getting along quite well now."

She and Jack knew it was time for their grandchildren to be a family with their father. And it was also time for her and her husband to resume their life. Their marriage, like that of thousands of other grandparents raising grandchildren, was tested. Most nights they just collapsed in bed in exhaustion, she recalled.

"We fought over our daughter," she added. "I blamed him for her behavior, though I must admit, he never said anything like that to me. There were times when I was so confused and angry I thought I was going mad. There wasn't much time or energy for one another.

"We still see the children often," added Agnes. "We take them on weekends, and we're involved with their activities. Susan is taking ballet, and it's doing wonders for her self-esteem, and she sings in the church choir too."

While Susan and Mae lived with their grandparents, they talked a lot about Jesus and His love. "Today, Susan is quite spiritual," said Agnes with a smile. "We have a bond. She calls me to talk. And she told me once, after we had settled into our life together, 'Grandma, you saved me.' "

Agnes and Jack are beginning to pick up their own lives again. They even have taken a vacation. "This experience has taught me how to come to grips with myself," said Agnes. "It's not easy to look at one's mistakes.

"I believe I've learned some of life's important lessons. I discovered that I could do something different with my grandchildren than I had done with my own children," Agnes said. "I often went into a rage with my own, and I didn't know why."

I asked about Jack and his place in all of this. "He was very supportive," she responded quickly. "He did not want it at first. He had just retired, but after the children were here awhile, he got called back to work. He got to escape!"

"I don't feel like something bad happened to me. This is life in this imperfect world," she added. "But I could not have done any of it without spiritual strength."

Making Connections

1. If you are raising grandchildren or know someone who is, look into a support group such as
   Grandparents Raising Grandchildren or start
   one in your area. Then others like you can come
   together and share the challenges as well as the
   joys.

2. Start a daily journal, jotting down your experiences and feelings as you raise your grandchildren. Write a letter to the Lord a couple of times
   a week and ask Him for His strength and grace
   in the areas you most need it. Be specific. He
   promised He would never leave us nor forsake
   us. Count on that as you open your heart to Him
   in prayer and writing.

3. Consider some new ways you might show your
   grandchildren your love for them. What specific
   actions can you take today that will demonstrate
   what is in your heart? Though your pain may be
   great, theirs is probably even greater.

WHEN DIVORCE OR DEATH SEPARATES

Lorraine wept openly as she confided the news she had just received. Her son Doug and his wife, Judy, were separating. They hoped to work things out, he had told his mother, but right now they needed time apart.

That conversation took place five years ago. Doug and Judy did finally work things out but not as Lorraine had hoped. They divorced three years ago, after several attempts to live together again.

Today, their two children, Annette and Michael, live with their mother a thousand miles away from Lorraine and her husband Bill. Judy has since remarried. Doug lives alone and sees the children for a month each summer and for a week during Christmas vacation.

"I used to see them every week," Lorraine said after a recent visit. "I miss them terribly. And they're growing up so fast."

Our friend Beth, also a grandmother, joined our conversation as we chatted over tea and a muffin. "I know what you mean," she told Lorraine. "Ever since Lou and Carol and the twins moved, I feel like part of my heart has been ripped out."

Beth meant to be supportive, I'm sure, but the two situations are entirely different. Beth's daughter and son-in-law, Mitch, are still married, and theirs was a job-related move because Mitch is in the military. Beth sees them twice a year, and she speaks with the children and their parents several times a month.

Unlike Lorraine, Beth does not have to contend with the complications of remarriage, step-grandparents on the "new" side, potential jealousy from the new spouse, or a change in family patterns such as holiday visits, gifts, phone calls, and so on.

Being separated from your grandchildren by geographic distance is not the same thing as being separated from them by death or divorce. If a person has not been through either one, according to those who share this experience, there is no real way of knowing what's involved.

Lorraine, however, knows firsthand. Her daughter-in-law's new husband wanted to limit the grandchildren's contact with her—"because Bill and I remind him of Judy's first marriage to our son, and he doesn't want to deal with that." Judy openly admitted this to Lorraine.

"Our former daughter-in-law could do something to help our situation," said Lorraine," but now that they're so far away, she does almost nothing.

"We've made various attempts—offering to fly the children here for a summer visit, meeting them halfway somewhere neutral, baby-sitting while she and her husband go on vacation, or whatever," said Lorraine. "But nothing's changed."

Lorraine and Bill are not alone. Each year, thousands of grandparents become the victims of their adult children's divorce. If, as statistics indicate, one in two marriages now end in divorce, that leaves a lot of grandparents on the sidelines.

A shift in the relationship between grandparents and grandchildren is inevitable as the adult children relocate, remarry, and reconstruct their lives in a new (and sometimes faraway) place and take their kids with them.

You may not have anything to say about those decisions, try as you might to change, fix, reason with, and even "understand" their point of view. The truth is, the outcome is out of your hands—and according to those I spoke with, that's the hardest part to come to terms with.

The death of an adult child may have similar effects on your relationship with your grandchildren—though the feelings about the event may be quite different. Instead of anger and frustration, grief and sadness may be the primary emotions at first. You may also be anxious and apprehensive as you look toward the future. Questions may flood your mind.

- What if the living spouse decides to remarry and moves away?

- What if the new spouse doesn't like me?

- What if I don't like the new spouse?

- What if the new spouse doesn't encourage my grandchildren's relationship with me?

- What if the new spouse doesn't love my grandchildren the way they deserve?

- What if the death (or divorce) results in the children coming to live with me? Can I handle it? Do I want to?

These are very real questions. And there are no pat answers. Each person needs to struggle through them on his or her own. Releasing the reins on this area of life, however, will be easier for some than others.

Eileen M., for example, said she had to drop all expectations when she heard that her daughter and son-in-law were divorcing. "For days, all I could do was cry. I didn't know what would happen next," she said. "I prayed that I wouldn't lose those darling children, but it was out of my control. I could write and call and invite them over, but if their mother said no, I had to accept it."

Eileen reflected on that for a moment, then added, "I think you have a little more say when the mother of the children is your own daughter. But if she's your daughter-in-law, it's a whole different story."

Not everyone would agree with that statement, however. One couple I spoke with said they have to be very careful around their own daughter. "We're afraid of alienating her. She's been a difficult person to live with for as long as we can remember," said Louann. "I feel like I'm always walking on eggshells around her."

Roger, her husband, nodded as his wife spoke. "Our daughter recently remarried, and we aren't too hot on this new son-in-law. Our daughter thinks he's wonderful, and she goes along with his way of doing things," Roger said. "We know he has more power over what happens in their house than we do, so we better not rock the boat.

"I kind of butter him up," Roger added, "asking him about his sailboat and things like that, just to keep the lines open, you know, but it's all for one purpose. To keep us in the picture. We don't want to lose our grandson."

Louann admitted that it took an enormous amount of effort to play this role, but she feels it's worth it. It sounds like a lot of hard work to me. I'm not sure anything is worth the price of one's personal integrity. But I haven't been down that road, and I don't know the situation they face.

What I have realized, however, in talking with various grandparents, is that there is no one way to handle the changes that come about because of divorce, death, and remarriage. Everyone involved gets hurt in some way.

Kathy and Bill said one of their sons has a precious little boy from a former relationship. But the parents are apart now, and the mother intends to keep it that way.

"She wrote a note saying she did not want our son in her child's life and that would mean giving us up too," Kathy said. "We respected her wishes, but it has been very painful. We do not see the little boy at all, but we pray for him daily—that he will come to know Jesus, as well as his earthly father, someday."

Some Positive Results

Joan and Lenard W. have a different viewpoint based on the experience of one of their adult children.

"Divorce has seemed to work better for our grandchildren than when their parents were together. They seem more relaxed and open with us," said Grandma Joan. "Of course they are not little kids anymore and that may be a factor in helping them handle the change."

She also said that she and her husband have coped with the divorce by maintaining the "desire to make it all work for the good of everyone." Joan and

Lenard have not interfered, and they have kept their support and love a constant in each person's life.

Elaine and Dave also had at least one positive result from the situation in their family. They actually had more contact with their daughter Vivian (Dave's natural daughter) and granddaughter Helen following Vivian's divorce.

"She seemed more free to relate to us and to allow us to get acquainted with Helen," said Elaine. "The divorce, however, also made it necessary for the two of them to move in with us for a year or so while Vivian got a job and saved enough money to become financially independent of us."

Edith said her daughter's divorce did affect her contact with her only grandson in a negative way at first. But then it changed for the better.

As a toddler, he was in and out of foster homes, following his parents' divorce. "It was a painful time for all of us," said Edith, reflecting back over two decades. "But when he was about three years old, our daughter finally obtained custody. Then we were able to see him often, and we grew very close. We have always been able to 'be there' for him, and he still knows that today."

Rely on the Word

Whatever the cause of separation—divorce, death, estrangement, or a broken relationship—those

I spoke with urged others in a similar situation to turn immediately to the Lord's Word. Although there are many good books on these subjects that offer practical and spiritual help, there is no comfort or advice or wisdom to compare with the Word of God. Garner those Scriptures that suit your situation and bring them to mind readily and often. Following are some examples to consider.

- *God is our refuge and strength, an ever-present help in trouble (Ps. 46:1).*

Take your worries to the Lord not to your grandchildren. Some folks have found it very helpful to keep a journal, especially during trying times. It's a good way to be honest before the Lord. I write to Him as my understanding Father and lay out my fears and worries. Then I listen for His response. Through this quiet time with my Lord, His Holy Spirit works to remind me of a Scripture passage that meets my need. The Spirit also strengthens me to take the appropriate action.

- *All your sons will be taught by the Lord, and great will be your children's peace* (Is. 54:13).

Focus on your grandchildren not on their parents. During times of crisis, it is the grandchildren who need our time and love and understanding more than anyone. Some grandchildren blame themselves for the events or feel overwhelmed by the changes they

146

can't control. Instead of wringing our hands or advising our adult children or bearing their burden for them, turn to your grandchildren and give them the unconditional love and stability they need.

One grandmother said all she could do was rock her two-year-old granddaughter after her daddy moved out. "What can you say to such a little one?" she mused. "Words don't help at that age. But she seemed to respond to my touch. I rubbed her back and cuddled and sang to her. I think I was her rock at that point, just as I needed the Lord to be my rock."

- *Everyone should be quick to listen, slow to speak and slow to become angry (James 1:19).*

Be a good listener. Ask the Lord to help you set aside your grievances and your grief as you listen to your grandchildren. Their perception of the situation and the consequences (especially the consequences to them) will differ from yours. It is important for them to put words to their feelings so they will not shut down emotionally. Avoid trying to "fix" or cure or redirect their words. Hold little ones as they talk or cry. And with older children, touch gently, take their hand, or simply look at them while they speak.

- *The Lord's unfailing love surrounds the man who trusts in Him (Ps. 32:10).*

Remain steadfast in your support and affection. Some grandparents rush in with love and help immediately after a death or divorce but then lessen their contact over the following months. But we may be the only solid anchor in the lives of our grandchildren for quite some time.

It's important for us to be consistent. That doesn't mean you must contact them every day or give up your own life or take them in permanently. Grandparents can communicate steadfastness and still have a life of their own. Phone or visit regularly. The frequency is not as important as the regularity. For example, suppose you take the children one weekend a month or overnight once a week—or whatever you and their parents agree on. Stick to that, and when you must change the schedule, be up front about it.

Be sure the children know that you are going to "be there" no matter what. Make sure they know you can be counted on. Sometimes that knowledge alone can go a long way toward building a secure relationship with you. They may not even take full advantage of what you offer, but just knowing they can if they want to can be healing in itself.

- *And He took the children in His arms, put His hands on them and blessed them* (Mark 10:16).

Spend time alone with each grandchild. During the transition months following a divorce or the death of a parent, children need individual comfort and care. This private time will give both of you the opportunity to open up, share, draw close, and express feelings and concerns that might be too personal to express in a group setting.

- *Give, and it will be given to you"* (Luke 6:38).

Encourage your grandchildren to express their emotions. While you are visiting with them, draw out their feelings. It's good to provide fun and laughter and a change of scenery, but some grandparents, hurting so much themselves, fear that if they or their grandchildren talk about the situation, it will have a negative effect. Actually, the opposite is true. The more a person can express, the less closed up and weary he or she will feel. You don't have to drag it out of them. Just make it easy for them to share, if they want to.

- *Dear friends, let us love one another, for love comes from God* (1 John 4:7).

Express your love consistently. Phone calls, surprise gifts, love notes, cards, and the words "I love you" are some of the simple ways you can affirm your grandchildren. Tell them you love them. Remind them that their parents love them. And most important, let them know that God loves them—that He, above all, will be there for them no matter what. Share some meaningful Scripture passages with them. Encourage older grandchildren to start a prayer journal or to search the Scriptures for the Lord's promises and then memorize four or five of them by saying them out loud each day.

- *Wisdom reposes in the heart of the discerning* (Prov. 14:33).

Avoid judging, taking sides, and name-calling. Your grandchildren have only one true mother and father, so don't do anything or say anything that would damage the relationship between them and their parents. Children are fiercely loyal. Children love their parents—no matter what. The Lord will settle debts and even up scores. We may have strong feelings about how the circumstances came about, but we don't have to share them in a way that will do more harm than good. God is the final judge.

- *The Lord is good, a refuge in times of trouble. He cares for those who trust in Him* (Nahum 1:7).

Make your home a safe haven during the stormy times. Children of divorce (or following the death of a parent) often lose their homes. They move away from their familiar neighborhood, attend a different school, must make new friends. But how wonderful it is if they can count on your home as a safe port—a place to sail into for a good meal, a loving conversation, a happy connection to the tradition and security they once knew.

Find ways, depending on your situation, to bring your children and grandchildren together in your home. Holiday dinners, birthday parties, summer picnics, etc., at your house can help them build a bridge between the new and old way of life.

- *I have come into the world as a light, so that no one who believes in Me should stay in darkness* (John 12:46).

Be a light on the hill. You may be the only contact with Jesus that your grandchildren have, especially when divorce occurs. Whatever else you may or may not be able to do, ask the Lord to help His light shine through you to your grandchildren. Look for opportunities to speak to them about Jesus, His promises, His Word in the Bible, and His presence in each one of us through His Holy Spirit. Richly share the forgiveness and love He won for us through His death and resurrection. Bible stories, videos with biblical messages, and stories of your own spiritual journey may provide the light that will lead them into the loving arms of the Lord Himself.

Making Connections

1. Go through the Scriptures listed in this chapter and write down one way that you could apply

them in your life in a practical way—whether or
not your family has experienced death or
divorce.

2. What do you consider to be your greatest
   strength in relating to your grandchildren during a difficult time? How might you expand on
   that?

3. What do you consider to be your greatest challenge in relating to your grandchildren during a
   difficult time? How might you overcome that
   challenge with the Lord's help?

10

COMMUNICATING THE TRUTH— WITH LOVE

"Do I have to stop this car in order to give you a spank?" I asked my granddaughter in a solemn voice. Johannah had been picking on her brothers in the back seat of my station wagon as we zoomed home from an outing at the park.

There was a moment of silence, and then a little voice popped up over the noise of the whizzing traffic. "Well," she said pausing, "how hard will the spank be?"

I couldn't keep a straight face. I lost it!

In moments such as this, every bit of wit and wisdom escapes me. The little munchkin wins. But there are other times when I cannot allow myself to lose it so easily. Grandchildren break an important house rule or they trample another person without apparent remorse or they disregard the boundaries we've set. Communicating the truth—with love—can be sticky. They're not our kids—but this is our house. We're not in complete charge of them—but we're in charge for the day or the week.

My daughter Julie and I have worked out one solution. When they're with me, what I say goes. *But* that takes into account that I know the way she parents them, the behavior she expects and enforces, and the manner in which she delivers consequences. We both believe continuity is important. And besides that, I deeply respect the way my daughter and son-in-law relate to their children.

On the other hand, I have my own *style*, and I feel free to express it, as long as I don't do anything that undermines or contradicts the principles Julie and Jon affirm.

This has worked well for us even though carrying it out is sometimes a challenge. For example, at home the children are allowed to jump on Mom and Dad's bed for a certain time each evening with supervision. At my house, my husband's and my bed is off limits to human jumping beans! But the kids still test me. And I continually test myself to see if I can be myself with them—without guilt—and still stand up for what is important to me, always communicating it with love.

Naturally, some things come easier than others. Spelling out rules about eating at the table or not climbing on the iron wall on the terrace are easier to talk about and enforce than speaking to a teenage grandchild about his drug addiction or to an adult child about questionable behavior that may influence a grandchild adversely (a gun hobby, for example, or smoking in the house or leaving children unsupervised even for a short time).

Tough Love

"We are having to be 'tough' with our son, Bob, because he seems to be frozen in depression," said Kathy with obvious sadness as her husband, Bill, nodded.

"He isn't even looking for work," she added. "His sense of worth seems to be completely gone. We have confronted him on his responsibility to his children and wife. And he does know that we care about him and love him no matter what."

Kathy and Bill have helped Bob and his family financially, as well as emotionally and spiritually. But they, like many other grandparents, agree it's always a challenge to communicate about difficult issues and still remain connected. Kathy readily admits that she needs more of the Holy Spirit's guidance.

Elaine, too, has faced the challenge of speaking the truth with love. She and her step-granddaughter Helen came toe to toe one day while Helen and her mother were living with Elaine and her husband Dave.

"Since I am Helen's step-grandmother," said Elaine, "we had to come to a conscious decision to treat each other as grandmother and granddaughter, especially since I had only seen her once before she and her mother moved in with us.

"One day, during an angry confrontation, Helen turned to me and yelled, 'You're not really my grandmother,' " Elaine recalled. "I put my anger and hurt aside because I felt this was an important moment that would have long-lasting consequences. I consciously lowered my voice and spoke slowly.

"I told her the way she felt about me would change from time to time. Sometimes she would feel full of love, and other times she would feel angry. But, I told her, being a grandmother is something that doesn't change. Either you are one or you aren't, regardless of how you feel," Elaine said.

"Then I told her that technically she was correct. I was her step-grandmother, since we weren't blood-related," Elaine continued. "I also reminded her that up to that point we had been relating as grandmother and granddaughter. It had been her choice to call me 'Grandmaw.' I told her she could choose to undo the relationship if she wanted to.

"I explained that I was ready to be her grandmother or not be, but whichever she chose, it would be for keeps and would not change based on feelings. I asked her to cool down before she made her decision," Elaine said.

Elaine recalled that Helen went to her room. When she came out she told Elaine she had decided she wanted her to be her grandmother. They hugged, and the issue never came up again.

But the challenge didn't end there. The toughest issue, according to Elaine, involved Helen's mother, Vivian. "She tried to be more of a friend to her daughter than a parent," Elaine said. "She wasn't strong enough on traditional parenting. She didn't expect obedience and respect.

"While they were living with us, she was gone most evenings and some weekends, leaving us in charge, but with no control over a very headstrong girl entering puberty," Elaine recalled.

"We tried to work through Vivian for most things. Otherwise her authority would have been completely undermined and Helen would have no one whom she felt she had to obey," Elaine said. "We were also sure Helen would play us off one another if she had the chance."

On one occasion, Vivian planned to be out of town for several days and assumed that Elaine and Dave would take care of Helen. "She did not even ask. I felt angry," Elaine added. "I also knew it would not work if I had no authority. So I told Vivian I would not baby-sit unless she told Helen she was to obey me while she was away."

It took some persuasion, but finally, both Vivian and Helen agreed. "And it worked," said Elaine, with a smile. "Helen was pleasant and obedient all the time her mother was gone. I never did have to be a 'just-because-I-say-so' authoritarian with her, but she knew that I could and would if necessary, and that was all it took. She seemed to like the security of having boundaries established."

Love and Tact

"One thing that has helped me in allowing my children to raise their children in their way," said Elaine, "is remembering how I felt years ago as a young mom. I was super-sensitive about how my mother and mother-in-law viewed my parenting skills. They usually had the wisdom to respect my wishes.

"On those rare occasions when they didn't, however, it was very painful, especially when my mother-in-law was critical of my parenting decisions in front of the children."

Elaine says with confidence that if she ever feels the need to speak to her children about their parenting, she'll plan it ahead of time. She will try to do it with love and tact and definitely not in front of the grandchildren.

To communicate with love is to connect with another human being. Elaine connected with Helen when she spoke the truth in love. She gave her granddaughter the opportunity to keep or change their relationship as grandmother and granddaughter. She was firm in her condition but loving in her approach. Helen must have known what she would be giving up had she closed the door on Elaine!

And Kathy and Bill took a brave step when they confronted their son about his financial responsibility. But they also assured him of their love for him no matter what. When people connect at this level of truth and love, both parties come away feeling supported and nurtured and respected. That opportunity is available to anyone willing to take it. It requires trust—trust in yourself that who you are is important enough to your children and grandchildren that they will not easily walk away from you just because you brought up some tough issues; trust in the other person that they are sturdy enough to hear from you in an honest and loving way; and most important, trust in God that He will direct your speech as well as the manner in which you speak.

But words alone are not enough. We need to put our love and support into action—behaving in ways that demonstrate our communication and display the deep love we feel for our grandchildren and their parents.

Show your love.

- Comment in a positive way on at least one thing you notice about the children, their parents, their home, meals, clothing, hairstyle, decorating, or anything else you see when you are together. If encouragement does not come easy for you, or if you tend to be critical by nature, ask the Holy Spirit to guide you in looking at what works instead of noticing what ought to be changed (in your opinion)! It's not enough to just have good thoughts. Show your love by communicating it to them.

- Bring a little gift or have a surprise ready when you get together. It can be as simple as a loaf of homemade bread or a few magazines you've saved that might be of interest to them. I pass on magazines to my daughter and her family, as well as coupons I think she can use, pictures for the kids to cut out and use in a home-schooling project, etc. Most of the time I don't spend any extra money. I'm simply sharing what I already have.

Speak your love.

- Make a habit of saying "I love you" to your grandchildren and their parents. My parents started a tradition in their family that my husband and I have continued. We end our phone conversations with "I love you." No one can hear those words too often. Find opportunities to express your love in words more often.

- Write out your expressions of love in letters and cards and notes. What a lift it is to receive an unexpected "love note" from a grandparent or parent. Or get creative. Make up a word scramble or puzzle or backward writing—all leading to the same message, *I Love You!*

Share your love.

- Reach out to extended family members. Include the "other" grandparents or step-grandparents, aunts, uncles, and cousins. Children thrive in the sanctuary of family. Let them see you sharing your love and they will feel free to do the same. Bring down the barriers so any family member who wishes to participate can do so. Take a deep breath right now and vow to take the initiative in your family. Plan a clan party or get-together. Make up your list and send out invitations. Don't worry about who in the family is speaking (or not speaking) to whom. It's your party. Invite those you wish. And be willing to accept whatever responses you get. The important thing is you made the first move. That's communicating—with love.

- Embrace your grandchildren's friends and

include their parents' friends in your sphere of interest. Ask about them. Invite them along on an outing or to dinner. Two families (friends of our daughters' families) are joining us this year for Thanksgiving dinner. There's enough love to go around.

Shelter your love.

- Stay close to the Lord. Take refuge in Him so you will have the spiritual resources you need to connect with your children and grandchildren through the tough times and to sustain you during the happy times.

- Seek the Holy Spirit's guidance at all times for all things. "Whether you turn to the right or to the left, your ears will hear a voice behind you, saying 'This is the way; walk in it' " (Is. 30:21).

Making Connections

1. Name one tough issue you'd like to communicate to your grandchildren or their parents— with love. Write down what you would like to say. Pray about it. Ask the Lord for wisdom and direction. Act on it as you feel He has led.

2. What new thing could you do this week to

demonstrate your love for your children and grandchildren?

3. Write a letter to your grandchildren's parents praising them for at least one or two positive things you've noticed about their parenting practices or about their family in general.

PART 4

LET GO
AND
LET GOD

11

GRANDPARENTING BY THE SPIRIT

"Grandpa, can I come in for a minute?" I asked, standing in the doorway of my grandfather's bedroom.

He turned from his desk and smiled with a twinkle in his blue Irish eyes. "Come in," he said, motioning me to his side.

"What are you reading?" I asked, noticing the old black book in front of him.

"The Bible," he said. "I'm reading the Bible."

Years later, when I became interested in studying the Bible for myself, I remembered the example he set, quietly and faithfully reading God's Word each day. I believe that was my first introduction to the Bible.

Now, as a grandmother myself, I have the opportunity to be an example to my grandchildren. It might come about in a different way but the opportunities for sharing are there nonetheless.

For example, one of my fondest memories of Noah, my first grandchild, is of waking up one morning in his parents' home and seeing the little fellow sitting at a play table near my sofa-bed. He was coloring away in a coloring book as he sang at the top of his voice, "Hosannah, Hosannah, Hosannah now we sing. ... " He couldn't have been more than four years old at the time.

"Come on, Magah," he called. "Wanna color with me?"

Before breakfast? I thought to myself. Then, just as quickly, I realized the opportunity I had right then, before anyone else awakened. Within minutes, I was up and dressed and sitting at his side, coloring and praising the Lord right along with him. It brings tears to my eyes just thinking about it.

How impressionable young children are, and how eager they are to build a close relationship with us, their grandparents. We, perhaps even more than their parents, have many truly golden opportunities to encourage and nurture their natural curiosity about God.

We can share the Spirit in play, in song, in story-reading, in skits, in conversation. It can be as simple as a few words.

"Magah, do you know the Lord?" asked Johannah one day as we played dolls.

"I sure do," I replied.

"Me too," she said. Then we continued our game.

Or it can be as comprehensive as a Bible lesson

complete with a dramatic presentation, a craft, and memorization of Bible verses.

It all has its place in the big picture. Discerning what to do and when to do it, however, is what makes the difference between a human grandparent with good intentions and a Spirit-filled grandparent who leans on the Holy Spirit for moment-to-moment guidance.

Spiritual Serendipity

When you walk by the Spirit, you're likely to be more spontaneous. For example, if you're reading your Bible and a grandchild interrupts you, don't close the book or shoo him away. Welcome him in as my grandfather did me. Pick out a verse just for him (or her) and even write it down on a little card he can keep. That card may end up as one of the treasures from you that he'll hold onto.

If you're playing dolls with your granddaughter, you may notice a way to include some spiritual serendipity as you play. The dolls could go to church, sing in the children's choir, or have a picnic with their vacation Bible school friends.

Teach the dolls a worship song. Let them lead a Sunday school class. As your grandchild playacts with you and the dolls, you'll see where she is with the Lord. You can build on that foundation as the Spirit leads you.

No Tacked-on Morals, Please!

Just as editors do not want writers to "tack on" a moral at the end of a children's story or build in a sermon-in-disguise, so, too, children do not want their grandparents to tack on a moral or a biblical truth to every conversation they have together. Kids turn away from such obvious stories, as well as from obvious adults who turn every visit into a Sunday school lesson.

I'm suggesting that we behave as the Spirit prompts us. That might be a Bible story one time and going on a hike the next. It might include a time of praise at the crack of dawn! Or it might be something as simple and human as comforting a crying baby or listening with understanding and sympathy to a frustrated teenager.

Consider how Jesus related to the people of His time. Sometimes He shared a meal with them, or fished, or attended a wedding feast. Other times He cast out demons and healed the sick and raised the dead. Jesus did what His Father in heaven told Him to do. He walked in the Spirit.

From the Heart

You may be squirming at just the thought of approaching the area of spirituality with your grandchildren. And if your grandchildren's parents are not

Christians or if they express disinterest or even disapproval, it's all the more challenging.

Perhaps you're still finding your way around the Bible and you don't feel comfortable or ready to share it with wiggly little kids or laid-back teens who may yawn in your face or adult children who don't welcome your viewpoint. Most of us can relate to facing such resistance.

Even if your grandchildren are being raised in a Christian home, you may still be apprehensive about entering an area of their lives that you feel should be reserved for their parents.

If any of these situations are true for you, I encourage you to ask the Holy Spirit for courage and wisdom about what part to play in the spiritual life of your grandchildren. I believe He does want us to be a light on the hill in their lives.

In Deuteronomy 4:9, the Lord encourages us to be involved with our children's spirituality without fear.

> Only be careful, and watch yourselves closely
> so that you do not forget the things your eyes
> have seen or let them slip from your heart as
> long as you live. Teach them to your children
> and to their children after them.

Grandparenting by the Spirit does not mean you have to attend church every Sunday, sing in the choir, or pray in secret for hours at a time. It's not about doing "stuff." It's not about performing. It's about being free in Christ.

> *It is for freedom that Christ has set us free. Stand firm, then, and do not let yourselves be burdened again by a yoke of slavery* (Gal. 5:1).

> *But if you are led by the Spirit, you are not under law* (Gal. 5:18).

Living in the Fruit

In Paul's letter to the Galatians (5:22–23), he says the fruit of the Spirit is love, joy, peace, patience, kindness, goodness, faithfulness, gentleness, and self-control. To express the fruit of the Spirit in one's life on a consistent basis, however, is a high standard for any person to aspire to. But even so, I believe it's important to ask the Holy Spirit to help us reach for that standard and to envision what it will be like when we are more able to express it—especially with our grandchildren and their parents.

- *Loving* grandparents are those who, according to 1 Corinthians 1:13, are patient and kind, do not take into account a wrong suffered, and are not jealous. Such a grandmother or grandfather is also free of guilt, for where love abounds, guilt cannot thrive. Grandparents who really love want the best for themselves, as well as for their loved ones.

- *Joyful* grandparents bring a glad heart to every situation—even when things look bleak or even hopeless. They see the Lord's hand in everything and on everyone. Such people do not look for what needs to be fixed or changed. They look at the blessings that already abound and give thanks for each one.

- *Peaceful* grandparents are those who know that all things work together for good for those who love the Lord. They are not critical or controlling. They don't blow up or sulk if things don't meet their expectations. They don't use words as weapons. Instead, they connect with their children and grandchildren in ways that lend support. They ask questions. They speak from their own experience. They share a piece of their heart instead of a piece of their mind!

- *Patient* grandparents can handle someone being late for dinner or forgetting to mail their birthday card on time. They share their feelings in a way that keeps their love flowing. They are not compelled to fix or change their children or grandchildren. They may ask questions, but they don't unload their raw feelings in the name of love. They trust God to finish the work He began in each one. And in the meantime, they enjoy their own lives.

- *Kind* grandparents remember that their grandchildren and their parents, like them, are human. They are still learning and growing and making mistakes. They know instinctively that it doesn't work to discount, diminish, or demean their loved ones with abusive words, gestures, innuendoes, or body language. On their birthdays, Christmas, and other special occasions, such grandparents express their love and attention in an individual way. They show their grandchildren they are among the most important persons in their lives. They've taken the time to get to know them. And because they know them, they care deeply and are willing and eager to express it.

- *Good* grandparents don't spoil the present by living in the past. They don't focus on their lives. They are more interested in hearing about the lives of their children and grandchildren. They are *good* people. They are good people to know, good to speak with, good to listen to, good to be with. And they help their grandchildren see and feel the good in all God's gifts.

- *Faithful* grandparents can be trusted. They say what they mean. And they do what they say.

They are true to God, true to themselves, and true to the people they are in relationship with. They are sometimes the only anchor in a grandchild's life. And they do not take that lightly. They can be counted on. They will "be there" no matter what. They will not bail out. They will not fail to hold up their end of a relationship. Children who have faithful grandparents are blessed indeed.

- *Gentle* grandparents rock an infant to sleep, snuggle with a toddler who awakens from a bad dream, pass out warm hugs to little kids who skin their knees or knock out a baby tooth. They listen to teens and young adults who need an understanding ear. They speak softly, move slowly, minister quietly.

- *Self-controlled* grandparents keep their own counsel. They increase their praise and eliminate criticism. They take their burdens to the Lord instead of to their children and grandchildren. They do not withhold their love until their children and grandchildren shape up, measure up, or live up to their expectations. They know God isn't finished with them yet—or with themselves, for that matter. They weigh what they say before saying it and consider what they wish to do before doing it.

Grandparenting without guilt is living in the Spirit, of the Spirit, and by the grace of the Spirit.

Making Connections

1. Write a prayer praising God for His Holy Spirit and for the guidance the Spirit provides in your life as a parent and grandparent. Be specific about the blessings you have received.

2. What fruit of the Spirit would you like to express more easily and more fully? Why? What specifically can you ask the Holy Spirit to help you do this week to make that change?

3. Go through the fruit of the Spirit listed in this chapter and write down your own definition of each one as it relates to you.

12

RELEASING YOUR GRANDCHILDREN TO THE LORD

During the course of writing this book, I received the loving support, through prayer and personal testimony, of so many Christian grandparents. You have met many of them in previous chapters. I'd like to conclude the book with their encouraging words to you, to me, and to one another, about how they have dealt with perhaps the most important aspect of being a grandparent: releasing our children and grandchildren to the Lord. I was very blessed by their words, and I hope you will be as well.

Pray—The Best Thing I Can Do

"I wish I could say I don't worry about them, but there are those times," says Bonnie, her voice trailing off mid-sentence. "I know the best thing I can do for them is pray. Each morning, I ask God's protection over my grandchildren and their parents."

Bonnie and her husband Warren, like many other grandparents, know the challenge that "releasing" often involves. Their daughter Sheri had trouble becoming pregnant. Then when she did, she miscarried several babies, including triplets. "I prayed a lot about these little children we all wanted so much," Bonnie said.

No wonder Andrew and Lindsey, who were born safely to Sheri and her husband, are today so precious to their parents and grandparents.

Warren and Bonnie also faced the challenge of completely releasing their second daughter, Pamela Eileen, to the Lord when she died at age nine following heart surgery.

"Our granddaughter has Pamela's middle name," added Bonnie. "It's fun to see little glimpses of our daughter in our granddaughter, Lindsey Eileen.

Let God Lead

Suzanne reminds other grandparents that our children are adults. "They're in control, we aren't. They have to live and learn just as we did. No one sets out to be a bad parent."

Suzanne admits it's not easy to let go and let God, but we must do it. "Let Him lead the way," she says with confidence. "And don't underestimate the power of prayer."

Release Control

"We all have to release control and worry

regarding our children and grandchildren," says Henry S. "We have surrendered ours to the Lord."

Henry made it sound easy, but I know it wasn't. His wife Betty elaborated on their situation.

"When our daughter Michele was two-and-a-half years old, she came within hours of dying of spinal meningitis," said Betty. "During the critical 24 hours when she was hovering between life and death, I read a booklet on prayer by Catherine Marshall. It included a chapter on relinquishment."

Betty then wrote her own prayer, relinquishing her daughter.

Dear Lord, I can't bear the thought of losing Michele after having had her for only two and half years. But since she actually belongs to You, please help me to accept Your will with grace and strength. I relinquish her to You now. Not my will, but Yours be done.

"In that desperate situation, as I petitioned the Lord regarding Michele, the Holy Spirit enabled me to totally trust Him—whatever the outcome," Betty recalled. "She was really *His* child, only loaned to us for a period of time—and He knows best because He is the omniscient Lord.

"That total release brought such peace that I was able to sleep soundly in the midst of that crisis. Since that spiritual landmark," said Betty with confidence,

"I acknowledge the Lord's absolute ownership of everyone and everything in my life. So my husband Henry, and my children, Mark and Michele, and now my little grandson Alex, are His."

Betty admitted, however, that practicing the spiritual principle of releasing others to God is a lifelong experience. "I am still learning how to view life and people through God's eyes," Betty said.

Listen

Joan W. sums up her experience in a few succinct words and phrases. "Pray. Talk to others. Read. Think. Mind your own business. No interfering. Listen."

Good simple advice! If each of us could do these few things, relinquishment might come about more easily than we could imagine.

Lean on the Grace of God

"We haven't had a problem releasing our grandchildren to the Lord," said Elaine and Dave, "possibly because we already had the experience of releasing our own children to Him."

Elaine reflected on a specific incident. "Years ago, I realized that if my younger son were ever to grow safely to maturity, it would be only through the grace of God.

"He did grow up," she added. "And it was by

God's grace. The Lord also brought him through a terrible car accident just a few years ago."

With that experience of God's grace still fresh in her mind, Elaine is confident that His grace will also sustain her grandchildren. "If I ever start to worry," she said, "I just look back on God's working in our lives."

Elaine said she also takes comfort in the beautiful words of an old spiritual,

I can't believe He brought me this far to leave me.

Ask for More of the Holy Spirit

"We need more of the Holy Spirit to keep from feeling discouraged sometimes. Releasing our children and grandchildren is an ongoing process," said Kathy, and Bill agreed. "Ask me how I feel from week to week, sometimes day to day. I know that God is in charge, but some days He seems closer than others, and then I can release my worry and concern more easily."

Kathy depends on God's promise that her faith will be strengthened as she studies His Word, but she admits that she needs to read the Bible more often.

"Walks on the beach help too," she said. "I can't see all that beauty and not know that God is up there and cares for each and every one of us."

Count Your Blessings

Mabel and Quimby admit they have a lot of blessings to count after raising their three children and then grandparenting six boys and girls. Today, when their grown grandchildren come to them for advice or encouragement, they give it freely.

"We tell them to count their blessings," said Mabel—advice she and Quimby have for anyone raising children or grandchildren. "Don't stop trying. Put things into the hands of the Lord. Listen to Him and obey."

Mabel says the words of John 13:34 say it best. "A new command I give you: Love one another. As I have loved you, so you must love one another."

Put Them in God's Hands

Julie H. admits that releasing her sons and grandchildren to the Lord has been hard. Since her husband's death, her children have helped fulfill her emotional needs. But when her son Jim and his family made plans to move to another state, it was a challenge to let go of them.

"I told Jim that I would never say, 'Please don't go,' even if my heart was screaming it! I know I can't control them," Julie says. "So I put them in God's hands. I say the name of each son, their wives, and my grandchildren every day in prayer and ask God to guide them, guard, bless, defend, keep, and save each one."

Leave the Carrots in the Fridge!

Granny Ace, as she likes to be called, releases her four grandchildren to the Lord by adopting a realistic stance. "It is not yesterday," she muses. "We hold not the reins. Comparisons are odious."

She gives her grandchildren and their parents plenty of room to live their lives. And perhaps because she has never lived near them geographically, it has been easier to release them.

"But I love them much," she says with conviction, "and that comes across. They also know that I love God. We converse less as they get older, but we still enjoy each other, and they know the deep inside love I have for them."

Granny Ace heads for "the basics" and urges other grandparents to do the same. As a Christian, she also rests in God's glorious name. She reminds us that "Children learn respect and they respond to truth, patience, understanding, and always, love. Leave the carrots in the fridge."

Share God

"It has been hard to release Alexis," says her grandmother, Dianna. Perhaps it's more difficult because she and her mother lived with Dianna for two years. At times, Dianna was a surrogate mother to her little granddaughter.

"But I have to keep the thought that Alexis is not my daughter," said Dianna. "As long as her mother, Caroline, does her best, I need to keep hands off and just be a grandma."

Dianna also stressed her commitment to pray for her daughter and granddaughter. She hoped that Alexis would always remember how she shared God with her through Sunday school and prayer and in their conversation.

Trust His Faithfulness

"Having been a Christian for 41 of my 84 years," says Edith, "I have learned that God is truly all-wise, all-knowing, all-powerful, and ever-present. He can do what we cannot, if we 'let go' and release our loved ones into His loving hands. He has proven Himself faithful over and over!"

Be Anxious for Nothing

The words and experience of other grandparents can be a great comfort when we face events we can't control, when worry grabs our minds, and fear tugs at our hearts. But when it comes right down to it, no grandparent, no adult child, no friend, no other human being can take the place of the Lord Himself and His words of comfort and encouragement.

I have told you these things, so that in Me you may have peace. In this world you will have trouble. But take heart! I have overcome the world (John 16:33).

We live by faith, not by sight (2 Cor. 5:7).

For God did not give us a spirit of timidity, but a spirit of power, of love and of self-discipline (2 Tim. 1:7).

In all these things we are more than conquerors through Him who loved us (Rom. 8:37).

Do not be anxious about anything, but in everything, by prayer and petition, with thanksgiving, present your requests to God (Phil. 4:6).

By meditating on these and other words of Scripture, and asking the Holy Spirit to make them *real* in our lives through action, we will demonstrate to our children and to our grandchildren that God is sufficient in all things, in all ways, for all time. The more we experience His sufficiency, the more we will express it. And in doing so we will be better able to release our children and grandchildren to Him, more fully realizing that eventually all things will pass away—hurt feelings, forgotten appointments, conflicting lifestyles, differing views, broken relationships, disappointments, fear, worry, disapproval, and misunderstanding will all pass away. Only the Word of the Lord will not pass away. He is faithful to do what He says He will do.

> *For I will pour water on the thirsty land, and streams on the dry ground; I will pour out My spirit on your offspring, and My blessing on your descendants* (Is. 44:3).

What better words to rest on than these, as we release our grandchildren, their parents, and ourselves to the Lord, trusting Him to do His perfect work in each one of us.

Making Connections

1. Write a letter to the Lord asking for His guidance and grace in releasing your children and grandchildren to Him. Be specific, especially if there are areas that are still difficult for you to let go of. If you feel you have already released them, ask for His continued provision and peace in this area of your life.

2. Write a letter to each of your grandchildren. Tell them you have released them to the Lord's care. Tell them your wishes for them as they grow

and develop spiritually. (You may wish to mail these letters or simply write them and keep them until the time is appropriate to share them.)

3. Write a personal psalm of worship and praise to the Lord for His blessing of grandchildren in your life.

ADDITIONAL READING FOR GRANDPARENTS

Bly, Stephen and Janet Bly. *How to Be a Good Grandparent*. Chicago: Moody Press, 1990.

Endicott, Irene M. *Grandparenting Redefined: Guidance for Today's Changing Family*. Edmonds: Aglow Publications, 1992.

Sonnenberg, Roger. *Celebrating Life as Grandparents: A Study Guide for Enriched Grandparenting*. St. Louis: Concordia, 1993.

Stoop, Jan and Betty Southard. *The Grandmother Book*. Nashville: Thomas Nelson, 1993.